The Plastic Effect®
How Urban Legends Influence the Use and Misuse of Credit Cards

The Plastic Effect
2013 Independent Publisher Living Now
Book Award Winner

Gold Medal Winner
Judged Best New Book in the Finance/Budgeting Category

Coconut Avenue, Inc. - Suggested Retail Prices

The Plastic Effect: How Urban Legends Influence the Use and Misuse of Credit Cards
Polly A. Bauer and Stephen Lesavich

Release Date:	December 14, 2012
Hardcover ISBN:	978-0-9837499-0-5
Hardcover List Price:	$27.95 US
Trade Paper ISBN:	978-0-9837499-1-2
Trade Paper List Price:	$24.95 US
E-Book ISBN (PDF):	978-0-9837499-2-9
E-Book List Price:	$19.95 US
Kindle ISBN:	978-0-9837499-3-6
Kindle List Price:	$9.99 US

Publisher's prices higher in other countries.

Prices subject to change without notice.

For current pricing information, please visit

Coconut Avenue, Inc. on-line: coconutavenue.com

PRAISE FOR

The Plastic Effect

"Polly A. Bauer combines her deep experience in the credit card industry with her passion for empowering and giving hope to those struggling with credit card problems in her new book, *The Plastic Effect*. A must read for all credit card holders."

-Janet R. Langenderfer, Senior Director, Amtrak

"Polly Bauer is the world's foremost expert on credit cards. If you want to grow your net worth, protect your portfolio and learn how to leverage the unparalleled power of credit, study this book like your life depended on it."

-Steve Siebold, Gove Siebold Group, author of *How Rich People Think*

"As an entrepreneur, being credit worthy is always a concern. Last year I paid an expert $4500 to teach me how to improve the credit for all my companies. I learned more in *The Plastic Effect* than I did from this so-called expert. This book could easily become the new 'financial bible' for business! Nobody knows more about credit than Polly Bauer."

- **Dr. Topher Morrison, Ph.D.**, Professional Speaker, International Event Host, and author of *Stop Chasing Perfection and Settle for Excellence*

"Large credit card balances and other financial concerns can be a constant source of individual and family related stress. As a health professional, I see how stress creates physical symptoms that can result in chronic health problems. The *Plastic Effect* is an effective handbook that allows readers to understand and use their credit cards more responsibly. Anyone who is under stress from credit card debt should read this book!"

- **Dr. Michelle Robin, D.C.**, Founder and Chief Wellness Officer (CWO) of, Your Wellness Connection healing center, and Author of: *Wellness on a Shoe String* and *The E Factor: Engage, Energize, Enrich – Three Steps to Vibrant Health.*

"*The Plastic Effect* is an empowering new handbook offering hope to those struggling with credit card related problems. This book will teach you what you need to know about credit cards, credit scores, credit reports and managing your credit card purchases more responsibly. A must read for anyone using a credit card!"

- **Colette Baron-Reid**, #1 Best-selling author of *The Map: Finding the Magic and Meaning in the Story of Your Life*, Radio Personality, Life Coach Trainer, Life Strategist, Motivational Speaker and Recording Artist.

"*The Plastic Effect* gives people more power over their financial lives by removing the veil of confusion that prevents them from taking charge of their financial affairs and helps them make decisions that can lead to both greater prosperity and peace of mind. In today's world, this is a must read for everyone!"

- **Sonia Choquette**, *New York Times* best-selling author of *The Answer is Simple*, Radio Personality

"*The Plastic Effect* is a springboard for reaching a new level of understanding of how credit cards are used and misused. An empowering and enlightening new book!"

-Jay Herring, Cyber-Security Professional and Author

"Not only is Polly Bauer an icon in the credit card business, she is a person with immaculate integrity who speaks and consults from the heart with power and passion! *The Plastic Effect* is a must read for anyone who is seeking how to truly understand, repair, control and manage the plastic in your life. To be aware is the first step in taking control instead of being controlled! Two thumbs up to Polly! From one who was once controlled and is now in control!"

- Roger Anthony, Founder and CEO of Crocodiles International, LLC, Motivational Speaker and Author of *Now I Understand, Tall Poppyship, 7-Steps to Mastery,* and *RINDIN the Puffer*

"*The Plastic Effect* provides practical and clear tips to guide us through our rapidly changing and increasingly complex plastic world. As a former partner in what was called a big eight accounting firm and 14 years international experience, I appreciate the financial wisdom that Polly A. Bauer shares with us in *The Plastic Effect.* This book is a must purchase and must read for everyone that wants to take charge of their financial future and understand how credit, and all related aspects in our increasingly plastic life, can be used to our advantage rather than being a source of worry and concern. Reading and applying these practical ideas can save us time, money, sleepless nights and put us in charge."

-James E. Stuebe, Javan and Associates, former Director, Latin American Division, Arthur Young & Co.

"*The Plastic Effect* is filled with the wisdom that can only come from a true insider. No one knows the credit card industry better than Polly. Buy this book and you will be richer for it!"

-John Paul Engel, Knowledge Capital Consulting

"The principles in *The Plastic Effect* have helped me more clearly understand my credit cards, my credit scores and my credit reports. This book is a phenomenal resource for information and tips for individuals at all levels."

- Amanda Cole, President, GadgitKids

"Polly Bauer knows more about credit cards than everybody I know combined. Polly and Stephen have developed *The Plastic Effect* to de-mystify urban myths about credit cards and credit scores. It is an excellent handbook that should be required reading for everyone."

- Magnes Welsh, Principal, Conscious Success Consulting

The Plastic Effect

How Urban Legends Influence the Use and Misuse of Credit Cards

theplasticeffect.com

POLLY A. BAUER, CPCS
speakerpollybauer.com

and

STEPHEN LESAVICH, PhD, JD
slesavich.com

®

Coconut Avenue ®
Chicago, Illinois USA

The Creative Avenue for Best Selling Authors ®

TABLE OF CONTENTS

TABLE OF CONTENTS

DEDICATION

- In loving memory of Warner Dahlberg.

Whose support, enthusiasm, affection, and persistence inspired this book, and so much more.

Polly A. Bauer

- To Zachary and Katherine.

Listen to your intuition and follow your passion always.

Stephen Lesavich

INTRODUCTION

With millions of people using (and misusing) credit cards every day, and credit card debt growing for many of us, it's time to stop and examine just what is motivating people in their credit card use. Among other factors, it's clear that many people are strongly influenced in how they use credit cards by what they learn from *urban legends*.

An urban legend is a second-hand story that supposedly happened to a real person. This story is repeated over and over. The story is told as actually being true and sounds just plausible enough for the listener to believe it. Closer examination usually reveals the legend to be just a story, like the tale of giant white alligators living in city sewers (which is, thankfully, untrue, as far as we know anyway).

Constant exposure to credit card-themed urban legends by consumers has produced a new social psychological phenomenon that has taken on a very interesting life of its own.

We call this new phenomenon *"The Plastic Effect."*

In this book, we have selected 25 of the most common urban legends that influence the use and misuse of credit cards. These urban legends are often responsible for generating and sustaining *The Plastic Effect*.

Why do you need to read this book? It is estimated that about 70% of all adults in the United

States have at least one credit card. It has also been reported that the average credit card holder in the US has not just one, but three or more credit cards, with an average of 3.5 cards per person.

In spite of the widespread popularity of credit cards, most consumers do not have a good idea of how credit cards are regulated, or what their rights and liabilities actually are when the cards are used or misused. In addition, most consumers do not understand how using or misusing their credit cards affects their health, their relationships, and their credit scores.

Volatile economic times, impulse shopping, health emergencies, the loss of a job, and a change in a life situation due to a marriage, divorce or a death are among the factors that can contribute to mounting credit card debt and the growth of *The Plastic Effect*. Many credit card users experience some (or even all) of these problems, and they can have major consequences.

Accumulating too much credit card debt affects many areas of your life, including your ability to pay your monthly housing, utility, food, and other costs. On top of the financial hardships, constant stress over financial issues can lead to chronic health problems. In addition, financial stress is also one of the main causes of arguments in a marriage or relationship. In short, more than just your bank account can suffer when you struggle with credit card misuse.

Your credit score is used to determine how fiscally responsible you are, and how much risk is associated with extending you credit or loaning you money. A poor credit score directly affects your ability to obtain additional credit, a loan for a vehicle, a mortgage, or even a new job. It also affects the interest rate you pay for borrowing money, as well as the rates for your insurance premiums. Making late payments or missing a payment on your credit cards or your monthly bills can significantly and negatively affect your credit score.

In short, handling credit cards the wrong way — and believing the urban legends out there about credit card use — can have adverse effects on your finances, your health, your relationships, and your ability to move forward with a positive financial outlook. *The Plastic Effect* can be a burden, but that's where we come in.

For each urban legend in this book, we provide an example to illustrate how the urban legend influences your perceptions. We then discuss the reality associated with each urban legend (some do have an element of truth) with respect to the use and misuse of credit cards, as well as its effect on credit scores. Additional information and resources are provided so you can further explore the topics associated with each urban legend. Finally, we offer a number of questions you can use to check on your own emotional state regarding the topics raised by each urban legend. These questions can be used to recognize and identify your own emotional triggers and allow you to make empowering choices when using your credit cards.

By the time you reach the end of this book, we predict you will have a better understanding of a number of important issues affecting the use and misuse of your credit cards. You will no longer be at the mercy of *The Plastic Effect* without knowing it. Your *credit-ability* also will be very different. We can see it *in the cards*! The plastic ones, at least.

Polly A. Bauer, CPCS
New Port Richey, Florida

Stephen Lesavich, PhD, JD
Chicago, Illinois

POLLY'S PEARLS OF WISDOM

Polly A. Bauer is considered by many to be one of the preeminent international experts in the credit card industry. With over three decades of experience, Polly is uniquely qualified to speak on credit card issues.

One of Polly's trademarks is wearing a string of pearls to business meetings and when she is giving speeches all over the globe as a professional platform speaker.

Pearls are formed in nature by live oysters and begin their existence as an *irritant* that cannot be removed. In response to the irritant, oysters create and secrete a substance to protect themselves.

Layer upon layer of this substance is accumulated around the irritation. This eventually creates a pearl — a gem that would not have existed without the irritant.

Credit cards are necessary *irritants* that cannot be removed for most consumers. However, by obtaining the right information, credit card irritants can be turned into beautiful credit card pearls.

For each urban legend in this book, Polly provides you with her unique insights and knowledge in the section of each chapter called "Polly's Pearls of Wisdom." The "Polly's Pearls of Wisdom" sections are indicated by the graphic shown at the beginning of this section. In some chapters, there's no good way to give you this information as a single pearl, so instead think of it as a string of pearls!

This valuable knowledge will give you the ability to take back control, changing what was an irritant into a priceless gem. You can use this information to overcome frustrations you may be experiencing from the use or misuse of your credit cards. "Polly's Pearls of Wisdom" will also help you add layer upon layer of valuable knowledge to your understanding of the use and misuse of your credit cards and your credit score.

Each "Polly's Pearls of Wisdom" section includes a deeper look at the urban legend topic. It also provides you with additional resources such as websites, addresses, and phone numbers that allow you to take the next steps to further explore the credit card and credit score topics associated with each urban legend.

THE PLASTIC EFFECT – DEFINED

The Plastic Effect is a new social psychological phenomenon associated with the use and misuse of credit cards. It is being driven in part by numerous *urban legends*.

There are five major factors that assist in the creation and circulation of the numerous urban legends that contribute to *The Plastic Effect*.

1. *The widespread daily use of credit cards instead of cash.*

Credit cards are very easy to use, widely accepted, and are used for almost every kind of purchase. Credit cards are used daily by millions of people to buy everyday items such as a cup of coffee, gasoline, and groceries..Big ticket items such as electronics, furniture, and appliances are also routinely purchased with credit cards.

A number of studies have shown that consumers who use credit cards to make daily purchases, spend more money each month than they do when making the same purchases with cash. This directly contributes to the accumulation of a significant amount of credit card debt.

2. *The enormous amount of misinformation available on the Internet.*

There are hundreds of millions of websites on the Internet, including countless blogs, information feeds, and video sites. Nearly any person can post any type of information.

Many Internet users still are under the assumption that anything published on the Internet has to be "the truth."

Numerous websites include information about credit card topics that is misleading, partially true, or just plain wrong. Unfortunately, this information is used directly by consumers when they are making decisions about the use of their credit cards.

3. *The extensive use of social media to instantly exchange information.*

Social media sites like YouTube, Facebook, and Twitter have made the exchange of information nearly instantaneous. It has become commonplace that a video, tweet, or other social media post will go "viral" and be viewed by millions of people in a very short period of time.

A recent study has shown that the social media site, YouTube has become a major outlet for news information. Large numbers of viewers trust information from YouTube as much as news information from conventional news sources.

This creates a problem for credit card related information (and other information) because YouTube is a site where anyone can post a video with essentially no filtering, editing, or fact checking.

4. *The prevalence of advertising.*

Advertising is everywhere — from television to billboards, in newspapers and magazines, and on mobile devices and tablets. Advertising can now be targeted directly at consumers based on websites visited and social media posts.

Advertisements can also trigger emotions in consumers that may cause them to make purchases based on these emotions. Advertisements are devised to affect you in both positive and negative ways, both of which can cause you to make poor purchasing decisions. These purchasing decisions directly affect credit card debt and change credit scores.

5. *The highly volatile economic times.*

The Wall Street crash of 2008 and the resulting financial crisis have contributed to a global recession with significant economic uncertainty. The ongoing recession in the United States is considered by many to be the worst financial crisis since the Great Depression of the 1930s.

Many factors caused this crisis; including the widespread availability of credit and credit cards, risk-taking by financial institutions, and financial deregulation. The aftermath of the crash has shown many negative effects. During the continuing unstable global economy, large numbers of people have lost their jobs, depleted their retirement savings, and exhausted their unemployment benefits. They were unable to pay their mortgages, credit card balances, and other bills.

Many consumers were forced to use their credit cards for their basic existence and accumulated large amounts of credit card debt. Many of these consumers missed payments and made late payments. Their accounts were sent to collections and many were forced to file bankruptcy.

As a result, the credit scores of such consumers fell by a large number of points. Lower credit scores have caused many consumers to feel depression, anxiety, increased stress, and other negative emotions. Unfortunately, many consumers' self-esteem and self-worth are directly affected by their credit scores. In an effort to make themselves feel better, many people further misuse their credit cards by purchasing unnecessary items or doing things they cannot afford.

Remember, *you are more than your credit score.* Empower yourself to make positive choices and overcome *The Plastic Effect.*

PLASTIC REACTIONS

For each of the urban legends we also include a section called *Plastic Reactions.* Many of our strongest reactions and impulsive decisions are a direct result of emotional triggers. There are both positive and negative emotional triggers.

Positive emotional triggers generate good feelings such as happiness, hope, and love. Purchasing decisions made based on such triggers can lead to the misuse of credit cards in many instances.

Negative emotional triggers generate bad and stressful feelings such as anger, depression, guilt, and helplessness. Negative emotional triggers more typically lead to the misuse of credit cards and result in more credit card debt.

Negative emotional triggers often lead to impulse purchases of products and services used for instant self-gratification. The products and services are used for easing the feelings associated with the negative emotions and may be used to fill an emotional void. Such negative emotional triggers disrupt the normal decision-making process.

You can avoid misusing your credit cards and increasing your credit card debt by becoming aware of your current emotional state and what feelings trigger your positive and negative emotions.

An important step is to check in on your emotional state frequently. Ask yourself questions such as:

- How do I feel right now?
- What is causing me to react this way?
- Why do I feel the need to buy this?
- Do I really need it?
- How will I feel after I buy it?
- How will I feel when I have to pay for it?

Empower yourself by forming a healthy new habit, and ask such questions before making any purchase with your credit card.

When emotional triggers cause you to make purchases with your credit cards, you give your power away to someone or something else. You become *disempowered* when you purchase something because of an emotional reaction.

You have a choice in how to react to your emotional triggers in these situations. Making a choice empowers you. By making a choice to not react to emotional triggers, you will help yourself to create a prosperous financial future for you and your loved ones.

In each *Plastic Reactions* section, we provide a number of questions for you to use to check your current emotional state for the topics raised by the urban legends. These questions can be used to recognize and identify your own emotional triggers, which will help you to make empowering choices when you use your credit cards.

If you write out answers to these questions, you may help yourself to better understand how to take control of habits surrounding your credit card use and empower yourself with knowledgeable decisions in the future.

WHAT IS A CREDIT CARD?

A *credit card* is a standard-sized plastic card used as a system of payment. A credit card is issued to a user by card issuer, typically a bank or other financial institution such as a credit union.

The credit card issuer sets up a *revolving account* and a *line of credit* for the user. The credit card holder is able to use the revolving account and the line of credit to borrow money to purchase goods and services from merchants. Most credit cards may also be used to obtain a cash advance.

A *line of credit* is a source of credit extended to the cardholder. The line of credit has a pre-determined spending limit or credit limit (e.g., $500-$25,000).

A *revolving account* is an account in which a cardholder is allowed to carry a continuing balance of debt, subject to pre-determined interest charges. Revolving accounts typically have a minimum payment requirement based on the account balance.

If the account balance is paid in full each month, no interest or fees are charged. If an account balance is not paid in full, interest is charged. The amount of interest is typically based on the entire account balance.

If a minimum payment is not made, or a payment is made after a due date, other fees are charged.

A credit card is different than a *charge card*. A charge card requires an account balance to be paid in full at the end of each month. Charge cards typically do not have any pre-set spending limits. However, if the balance is not paid in full at the end of the month, then penalty fees will be assessed, additional charges may be restricted, and the account may be canceled.

A credit card is also different from a *debit card*. A debit card is similar to a credit card in the way it is used as a payment for goods or services, but it withdraws funds already deposited in a bank, checking, or brokerage account. Debit cards withdraw cash from the associated account instead of borrowing money, and do not incur additional debt for the consumer.

Unlike credit and charge cards, payments made using a debit card are immediately removed from the cardholder's account. Most debit cards can also be used at Automated Teller Machines (ATM) to withdraw cash from the cardholder's account. Many merchants also allow the cardholder to withdraw cash from their bank account at the time a purchase is made (the "cash back" option when you make a debit purchase at a store).

There are multiple types of credit, charge, and debit cards that can be used by both individuals and corporations.

Polly's Pearls of Wisdom: When traveling, be careful using a debit card for transactions like car rentals and hotel stays. Car rental agencies that accept debit cards will usually require a deposit that will put a "hold" on funds in your account to cover potential damages to the vehicle, in addition to the amount of the car rental. The amount of the funds on hold will not be available for you to spend until the rental car is returned undamaged and the final bill is paid. The money on hold is being kept in a "holding pattern," so even though it's your money, you can't spend it while it's on hold without potentially overdrawing your account.

Hotels will also put your funds on hold for the amount of the expected charges that will be incurred during your stay, and that amount may exceed the final bill you receive from the hotel. This means that, if you book a hotel room for three nights at $100 per night, the hotel may put a hold of, say, $500 on your account to cover the things you <u>might</u> charge to the room during your stay, like room service and concierge service. If you don't actually charge anything else to the room, you'll get billed just for the $100 per night for your room when you check out, but before the bill is settled, the extra $200 the hotel puts on hold won't be available to you to spend.

If you're going to use your debit card this way, you should plan accordingly. Make sure you have enough cash available in your account to cover your expenses plus the amount of money that will be on hold while you're traveling. If you plan to pay for the car rental or hotel room with your credit card, use that card to initiate the transaction so that the cash in your account that is associated with your debit card is available to you during your travels.

WHAT IS A CREDIT REPORT?

A *credit report* is a record of your credit activities created by a *consumer/credit reporting agency* (CRA). Your credit report lists all accounts for which money has been lent to you and credit extended to you.

Your credit report includes financial information (e.g., your mortgage, loan, and credit card account balances), and your payment history (including on-time and late payments). Also included is a list of any legal actions you have taken (e.g., declaring bankruptcy, having debt canceled, etc.). Legal actions that have been taken against you (e.g., collections actions initiated against you, a repossession action initiated against you, or a legal judgment or tax lien recorded against you, etc.) are also listed in your credit report.

The most common type of CRA is a *credit reporting bureau*. The three major credit reporting bureaus in the United States are *Equifax, Experian* and *TransUnion*. The current contact information for these three credit reporting bureaus is included in Appendix A.

The credit reporting bureaus routinely collect and record information from lenders who have loaned you money, credit card issuers, and other financial institutions who have extended credit to you.

A large number of credit reports include errors. The credit reporting bureaus obtain and record huge amounts of information on a daily basis. It is common for mistakes to be made by the credit reporting bureaus. It is also common for the entities reporting information to the credit reporting bureaus to make mistakes.

In the United States, the Fair Credit Reporting Act (FCRA)[1] gives you the right to contact the credit reporting bureaus and have errors removed from your credit report. The FCRA prohibits the credit reporting bureaus from reporting inaccurate, incomplete, or unverifiable information. In 2003, the FCRA was revised by the Fair and Accurate Credit Transactions (FACT) Act[2] to allow consumers to obtain a free copy of their credit report from each of the three major credit reporting bureaus once per year.

Credit reports obtained from each of the three major credit reporting bureaus include similar categories of information, but each bureau presents the information in different formats. The order in which the information is listed also varies, as do the section headings and the layout of the reports. The information contained in each version of your credit report may also differ because not all creditors report information to all three of the major credit reporting bureaus.

The information contained in your credit report will generally fall into the following categories:

- Personal Information
- Account Information
- Public Records/Legal Records
- Adverse Accounts
- Satisfactory Accounts

- Inquiries Shared Only With You
- Inquiries Shared With Others

The "Personal Information" section includes the following types of information:

- Your name and other names associated with you (e.g., married and maiden names, and known aliases)
- Social Security number
- Date of birth
- Current and previous addresses
- Current and previous telephone numbers
- Employment history

The "Account Information" section provides a key to help you understand the payment history information included in your credit report.

The "Public Records" section includes a list of civil legal judgments that may have been obtained against you. Such entries remain on your credit report for seven years. It is not the practice of the three report bureaus to report criminal convictions.

The "Public Records" section also includes any bankruptcies you may have filed. Such entries remain on your credit report for seven to ten years, depending on what type of bankruptcy was filed.

The "Adverse Accounts" section includes accounts that creditors consider to be unfavorable. Such entries remain on your credit report for seven years.

Each entry in the "Adverse Accounts" section includes information such as:

- Creditor name and contact information
- Date updated and date paid
- Credit limit
- Original balance and past due balance
- Payment status
- Account type and responsibility
- Date opened and date closed

Table 1 provides a sample "Adverse Accounts" entry from a sample credit report for a credit card.

Table 1. Adverse Accounts Entry	
OUR BANK Credit Card	Information
1234 Main Street Chicago, IL 60603 USA (800)OUR-BANK	**Balance:** $1,234 **Date Updated:** 08/27/2012 **Past Due:** $99.34 **Pay Status:** 120 days past due **Account Type:** Revolving **Responsibility:** Individual **Date Opened:** 07/07/1986

The "Satisfactory Accounts" section includes accounts creditors consider to be in good standing (i.e., no adverse information such as late payments, missed payments, or overdue balances). Such entries remain on your credit report for seven years.

Each entry in the "Satisfactory Accounts" section includes information such as:

- Creditor name and contact information
- Date updated
- Original balance
- Credit limit
- Payment status
- Account type
- Responsibility
- Date opened and date closed
- Date paid

Table 2 shows a sample "Satisfactory Accounts" entry from a sample credit report for a utility company.

Table 2. Satisfactory Accounts Entry	
My Electric Company	Information
5678 Volt Street Chicago, IL 60603 USA (800)ELC-TRIC	**Balance:** $0 **Date Updated**: 08/27/2012 **Past Due:** $0 **Pay Status:** Current **Account Type:** Open **Responsibility:** Individual **Date Opened:** 11/11/1981

Table 3 provides a sample "Inquiries Shared Only With You" entry from a sample credit report for a credit card company creating a list of pre-approved credit offers. Such an inquiry is called a *soft inquiry* or a *soft pull*. A *soft inquiry* typically remains on your credit report for six months. These credit inquiries appear on your credit report when you receive it, but are not shared with any other party viewing your credit report. A soft inquiry does not affect your *credit score* (see **Urban Legend 1**).

Each "Inquiries Shared Only With You" entry includes information such as:

- Requestor name and contact information
- Request date

Table 3 shows a sample entry for a person who will be considered for a pre-approved credit card from the bank YOUR BANK.

10

Table 3. Inquiries Shared Only With You Entry	
YOUR BANK MYD Card	Information
9123 Main Street Chicago, IL 60603 USA (800)MYD-CARD	**Request Date:** 08/27/2012

Table 4 provides a sample "Inquiries Shared With Others" entry from a sample credit report for a credit card company. Such an inquiry is called a *hard inquiry* or a *hard pull* and remains on your credit report for two years. A hard inquiry is an actual inquiry from a creditor that is used to determine your *creditworthiness.* Every hard inquiry directly affects your *credit score* (see **Urban Legend 1**).

Each entry in the "Inquiries Shared With Others" section includes information such as:

- Creditor name and contact information
- Request date
- Inquiry type
- Loan type and loan amount (if installment loan inquiry)
- Permissible use

Table 4 shows a sample entry for a person applying for a new card from the bank OUR BANK.

Table 4. Inquiries Shared With Others Entry	
OUR BANK MASCARD	Information
5678 Main Street Chicago, IL 60603 USA (800)MAS-CARD	**Request Date:** 08/27/2012 **Inquiry Type:** Joint **Permissible Use:** New Credit Card Application

The information and fields shown in Tables 1 - 4 are samples only. Remember, your credit report from each of the three credit reporting bureaus will include similar types of information, but the individual fields may be named differently and presented in different orders. The information reported to each credit reporting bureau may vary because not all creditors report to all three credit reporting bureaus.

Polly's Pearls of Wisdom: As hard as I've tried, there's no good way to give you this information as a single pearl, so think of it as a string of pearls! You need to be aware that under US Federal Law[3], you can request a free copy of your credit report from each of the three major credit reporting bureaus once per year.

Information on obtaining your free credit reports is available from the Federal Trade Commission (FTC) online at: (www.ftc.gov/freereports).

Your free annual credit reports are available online at one central location at: (www.AnnualCreditReport.com) or by calling (877)322-8228. You can also request your free credit reports by downloading the "Annual Credit Report Request Form" from the FTC website and mailing it to: Annual Credit Report Request Service, P.O. Box 105281, Atlanta, GA 30348-5281.

Since you are entitled to one free credit report from each credit reporting bureau, consider ordering one of your credit reports from one of the credit reporting bureaus in each four-month period during a calendar year. This way, you can monitor your credit for free throughout the year.

Each credit reporting bureau may report different information, and may include different errors, so take advantage of your legal right and request your credit report from all three credit reporting bureaus.

Review the information on each of your credit reports and take action to correct any errors you find. If you find any errors in your credit report, you can dispute the errors electronically directly from your free credit report. The three credit reporting bureaus each provide you with a method to initiate a dispute directly from the display of your free credit report. You can also dispute any errors you find in writing.

The FTC publishes a document entitled *"FTC Facts for Consumers – How to Dispute Credit Report Errors"* that is available online at: (www.ftc.gov/bcp/edu/pubs/consumer/credit/cre21.shtm).

The FTC document lists the necessary steps you must take, and includes sample letters to send to the credit reporting bureaus and other creditors.

In general, at least two steps are required for every incorrect entry you find on your credit report. You must write to both the credit reporting bureau that reported the error, and the appropriate creditor. In these letters, you must indicate which entry you want to dispute as inaccurate, and explain in detail why you think the entry is inaccurate.

For example, consider the "Adverse Accounts Entry" shown in Table 1. Suppose you reviewed your credit report and saw this entry. Also, suppose you do not have a credit card issued by OUR BANK.

It is necessary to correct this error immediately because it is an adverse entry and will negatively affect your *credit score*. To remove this entry, first, you must write to the appropriate credit reporting bureau, and explain that you do not have a credit card issued by OUR BANK. You must request the credit reporting bureau completely remove the entry. Second, you must write to OUR BANK, request they explain why the credit card entry was entered under your name, and request the error be immediately corrected with the credit reporting bureau.

If your credit report includes any negative information that is indeed accurate, only the passage of time will remove the entry from your credit report. The amount of time varies (depending on the type of information) from two years (for normal credit inquiries by creditors) to seven years (for negative information such as missed or late payments, etc.) to ten years (for certain types of bankruptcy and other negative information).

Unfortunately, the credit reporting bureaus are not required to provide you with a free credit score when you request a free credit report. In fact, the free credit reports do <u>not</u> include your current credit scores. How to obtain a free credit score will be discussed in the next section.

WHAT IS A CREDIT SCORE?

A *credit score* is a number calculated from credit information on your *credit report* and indicates your *creditworthiness*. *Creditworthiness* is how likely you are to repay any money lent to you. Like it or not, decades of research have shown that a person's credit score can be used directly to predict risk in underwriting of both credit and insurance.

The credit reporting bureaus and most major financial institutions (such as credit card issuers, banks, and mortgage companies) have developed their own credit scoring models. These proprietary credit scoring models are kept secret and are never published.

As a result, any discussion of credit scores, including those presented in this book, is always a *best guess* estimate. Your credit score is directly related to your individual credit and debt activities.

One of the most popular and widely known credit scores is the *Fair Isaac Corporation* (FICO) credit score. FICO scores are used in the automobile, banking, credit card, mortgage, and retail industries. About 90 percent of all lenders use FICO credit scores to determine creditworthiness.

When a *credit score* is discussed, it is typically a FICO credit score. For simplicity, throughout this book, any discussion of credit score will be with respect to FICO credit scores and the associated FICO credit score identifiers and number ranges.

In reality, your credit score is actually three separate credit scores, one from each of the three major credit reporting bureaus: *Equifax*, *Experian*, and *TransUnion*.

Each of the three credit reporting bureaus uses a slightly different range of numbers for credit scores. Your credit score from the three credit reporting bureaus will vary by a number of points because the models for the three credit scores were developed separately, and different items may be reported to each of the credit bureaus.

Under the FICO credit score modeling system, your credit score is a number from 300-850.

The higher your credit score number, the less risky you appear to a lender that is considering lending you money. The higher your credit score, the more access you will have to opportunities to obtain credit, a loan, a mortgage, a lower interest rate, etc.

A credit score ranges from 300-850. The credit score categories are shown in Table 5.

Table 5. Credit Score Categories	
Excellent	**760-850**
Great	**700-759**
Good	**660-699**
Fair	**620-659**
Poor	**580-619**
Very Poor	**300-579**

No matter what credit scoring model, scoring ranges, or nomenclature is used, your credit score is calculated using data from your credit report in five different categories. The credit score components are listed in Table 6.

Table 6. Credit Score Components	
Payment History	**35%**
Credit Utilization	**30%**
Length of Credit History	**15%**
Types of Credit Used	**10%**
New Credit Obtained	**10%**

Your *payment history* including your on-time and late payment information, accounts for 35 percent of your credit score.

Your *credit utilization* accounts for 30 percent of your credit score. Credit utilization is a ratio of how much debt you owe to how much credit you have available. A low ratio is considered more desirable to lenders. This factor includes your credit utilization for each of your credit cards individually and an aggregate credit utilization for all your credit cards together.

The *length of your credit history* accounts for 15 percent of your credit score. Your credit history includes the dates you opened your credit accounts and the time that has elapsed since the last activity on each account.

The *types of credit* you use accounts for 10 percent of your credit score. The types of credit include *revolving* and *installment* credit accounts.

A *revolving* credit account is an account where a user is assigned a pre-determined credit limit and the user is able to borrow varying amounts of money from the account. Credit cards are a common type of revolving credit account.

The user makes periodic payments on the amount borrowed but does not have to pay back the full amount borrowed each month. Revolving credit accounts typically charge a service fee and/or interest on the amount borrowed.

Installment credit is a type of account that includes a fixed number of required payments at a fixed amount including interest. Installment credit interest is typically charged at an annual percentage rate (APR). Auto loans, mortgage loans, and student loans are examples of installment credit accounts.

The *amount of new credit* accounts for 10 percent of your credit score. The amount of new credit includes new credit inquiries (e.g., hard inquiries) and the number of recently opened new accounts.

Polly's Pearls of Wisdom: Credit scores are used by lenders to determine who qualifies for credit, and what the credit limit and interest rate should be.

The credit reporting bureaus are not required to provide you with a *free credit score* with the free *credit reports*. The free credit reports do <u>not</u> include your current credit scores.

So what is the best way to obtain your current credit scores for free?

There are many websites that report to offer "free credit scores." However, most require that you input credit card information and sign up for free trial offers that require monthly fees if they are not canceled within a specified time period. There have been many consumer complaints filed against sites that claim to provide free credit scores.

A large number of the complaints include those related to consumers having a very difficult time trying to cancel credit report and credit score services either from the company's website or on the phone, and those related to hidden fees and charges buried in fine print in an electronic agreement used during the sign-up process. So beware!

Before signing up for any free credit score or free credit report offers, check with the FTC (www.ftc.gov), the Federal Reserve (www.federalreserve.gov), or the Better Business Bureau (www.bbb.org) for more information about the company. You can also check out the major news service websites for information about current credit score and credit report scams at sites such as:

CNN Money (www.money.cnn.com),
MSN Money (www.money.msn.com),
FOX Business (www.foxbusiness.com), and other sites.

As of the date of publication of this book, you have to visit at least three different websites to obtain all three of your credit scores from the three credit reporting bureaus. However, you can do a quick search engine query to determine if anyone is now providing a website that allows you to obtain all three of your credit scores for free.

As of the date of publication of this book, there is currently no way to obtain your **Equifax** credit score for free without paying or signing up for a free trial offer. However, you can do a quick search engine query to determine if anyone is now offering a free Equifax score before paying a fee or signing up for a trial offer.

To obtain your Equifax score, you must purchase it or sign up for a free trial that includes entering credit card information.

You can purchase your Equifax credit score for a fee (e.g., $15.95) directly from Equifax (www.equifax.com). The fee currently includes an Equifax credit report and a personal analysis of your credit situation.

You can also get your Equifax score for free by signing up for a 30-day free trial credit card score offer at Go Free Credit (www.gofreecredit.com). Remember to cancel your free trail before the 30-day free trial expires to avoid being charged.

You can determine your **Experian** credit score for free at Credit Sesame (www.creditsesame.com). Credit Sesame also provides analytic tools that analyze your current credit and debt profiles, and provides personal financial advice.

You can determine your **TransUnion** credit score for free at Credit Karma (www.creditkarma.com). Credit Karma also provides tools that allow you to compare your credit score to others based on a number of factors, and tools to assist you with managing your personal finances.

As of the date of publication of this book, there is currently no way to obtain your **FICO** score for free without paying a fee or signing up for a free trial offer. However, do a quick search engine query to determine if anyone is now offering a free FICO score before paying a fee or signing up for a trial offer to obtain your FICO score.

You can obtain your FICO score for free from My FICO (www.myfico.com) by signing up for a 14-day free trial credit card offer. Remember to cancel your free trial before the 14-day free trial expires to avoid being charged.

You can also find FICO score estimators from My FICO (www.myfico.com) and What's My Score (www.whatsmyscore.org) that provide *estimated* FICO scores based on your answers to ten or more questions. Got Credit (www.gotcredit.com) and Free Credit Score (www. freecreditscore.com) also provide general credit score estimators.

Such tools are valuable if you are trying to understand how making different financial decisions may affect your FICO credit score or other credit scores. Keep in mind these sites provide estimates only, and your actual credit score is directly dependent on your own credit report and your own decisions.

URBAN LEGEND – 1

Applying for a new
credit card will not
affect my credit score.

Urban Legend Number 1: I applied for and received a new credit card. I have a good credit score with all three credit bureaus. My credit score will not be affected because I received the new credit card.

The Reality: *False.*

When you apply for any new credit card from a credit card company, the credit card company does a *credit inquiry* on you. The credit inquiry is a notation on your credit report that someone has requested your credit history. The credit inquiry is used to determine your *creditworthiness*, that is, how likely you are to repay any money lent to you.

There are two types of credit inquiries: *soft inquiries* and *hard inquiries*. *Soft inquiries* do not affect your credit score. *Hard inquiries* have a direct effect on your credit score.

Soft inquiries or *soft pulls* include such events as a person checking their own credit score; credit checks by employers; and the creation of list inquiries by credit card companies, mortgage companies, etc., to create lists of pre-approved applicants.

When you apply for a credit card, the credit card company does a *hard inquiry* on you. The *hard inquiry*, also called a *hard pull*, is a review of your credit report by a third party such as the credit card issuer.

This hard inquiry directly affects your credit score and usually causes it to go down. About 10 percent of your credit score is determined by the number of hard inquiries on your credit report.

Why does the hard inquiry cause your credit score to go down? Credit score rules consider anyone applying for new credit (e.g., a new credit card, loan, or mortgage) to be incurring additional debt. That increases the financial risk associated with extending additional credit or lending money to that person.

Numerous hard inquiries are also viewed as a potential indicator that a person is attempting to expand his/her debt limits, or may be experiencing financial problems, both of which increase the risk that the person may not be able to pay back any additional money lent to him/her.

Polly's Pearls of Wisdom: The impact of a *hard inquiry* on your credit score varies depending on your credit history.

A single hard inquiry typically reduces your credit score by up to five points for the six months following the hard inquiry. A hard inquiry typically remains on a person's credit report for about two years.

Did you know that other common activities also result in hard inquiries that can affect your credit score? Some of these are: getting a new cell phone or changing your cell phone carrier; connecting utilities such as electricity, natural gas or cable television; opening a new bank account; opening a trading or retirement account with a broker; signing a lease to rent an apartment; and going through a divorce.

If you are planning to apply for a mortgage or a loan for a large purchase (e.g., automobile, boat, motorcycle, etc.) in the next one to two years, you should try to limit any activities that result in multiple hard inquiries.

Multiple hard inquiries in a short time period have a negative effect on your credit score and can result in you either being placed in a higher risk category for which you will pay a higher interest rate, or having your mortgage or loan application denied.

Plastic Reactions:

- Why did you apply for a new credit card?
- Did you have a specific purchase in mind when you applied?
- Were you calm or anxious when you completed the application?
- How do you feel knowing that applying for a new credit card will affect your credit score?
- How closely do you monitor your credit score?

URBAN LEGEND – 2

Pre-approved credit card applications indicate I have good credit.

Urban Legend Number 2: I have received an unsolicited *pre-approved* application in the mail for a new credit card from a credit card company. I am *guaranteed* to receive the new credit card from the credit card company because I am *pre-approved*.

The Reality: *False.*

Credit card companies routinely buy lists of potential customers from the three major credit bureaus. The credit card companies use the lists and other demographic information to target individuals that meet a desired credit score level, income level, or other desired threshold criteria. Typically, the individuals on the lists are then targeted in a mass mailing with a paper application or an application sent electronically (e.g., via e-mail).

A majority of individuals who respond to the mass mailings are eventually approved and receive the new credit card as a result of the pre-approved status.

However, the pre-approved status does not mean you are *guaranteed* to receive the credit card you are applying for. The fine print on the application almost always says your approval for the credit card will be determined based on information you submit on the pre-approved application as well as the information on your current credit report.

Your pre-approved status was a result of a *soft inquiry* by the credit card company to create a list of candidates. If you apply for the pre-approved credit card, that will result in a *hard inquiry* by the credit card company and your credit score will drop by a few points (see **Urban Legend 1**).

Numerous individuals receiving a pre-approved application appear on the list as the result of some sort of mistake and may actually have a poor credit score.

In addition, events occurring after the credit card company's lists were prepared can result in someone with a pre-approved application not receiving a new credit card.

For example, after receiving the pre-approved application you may have recently missed or made late payments, applied for one or more new credit cards, or applied for a new loan or mortgage. You also could have had a change in your personal status (e.g., marriage, divorce, or the death of a spouse), or a legal judgment recorded against you.

As result of such events, you may be denied a new credit card even though you applied for the new credit card with a pre-approved application.

Polly's Pearls of Wisdom: Many *pre-approved* applications include other offers to further entice you to apply for the new credit card. What attracted you to this offer? Was it a zero percent interest rate, rewards like air

miles, or a higher credit limit? Be sure to read the exact
words and the fine print.

Be aware of words such as "as low as," "up to,"
and "if you qualify," which are not definite contractual
terms. Even though you are *pre-approved*, you may not
qualify for the best terms or the lowest interest rate
because of your current credit score.

Also, consider the total costs associated with
obtaining and using the new credit card. Compare the
offer closely with the terms and costs of your current
credit cards. The new credit card may have a higher
annual fee, a higher interest rate after the promotional
period, higher late fees, or higher cash advance fees than
the credit cards you currently have.

There are a number of websites on the Internet to
compare credit card offers, including pre-approved
offers. The sites offer side-by-side comparisons of the
offers, and many provide independent ratings of the
credit card issuers and consumer reviews. You can use
such sites to compare your current credit card to a pre-
approved credit card offer that you are considering.

Websites to compare credit card offers include:
Compare Cards (www.comparecards.com),
Credit Cards (www.creditcards.com), and
Card Hub (www.cardhub.com).

If you are not interested in applying for new credit
cards, you should routinely shred or otherwise destroy
the pre-approved applications. This will help prevent
identity theft and other types of fraud from "dumpster

divers" or others who may try to sort through your garbage.

You can also stop receiving the pre-approved applications altogether by opting-out. To *opt-out*, you are required to send a letter to one or more of the three credit reporting bureaus, and ask to be removed from any lists they generate for pre-approved applications. The current contact information for the three credit bureaus appears in Appendix A.

The three credit bureaus also offer a toll-free number that enables consumers to opt-out of all pre-approved credit card offers. One phone call to (888)5OP-TOUT removes your name from such lists for all three credit bureaus.

Additional information for opting-out of receiving new credit card applications is available from the Federal Trade Commission (FTC). You can reach the FTC by calling (877)FTC-HELP.

The FTC refers to pre-approved offers as "pre-screened" offers. The FTC website (www.ftc.gov) refers consumers to the website Opt Out Prescreen (www.optoutprescreen.com). This is the official Consumer Credit Industry website to opt-out of receiving pre-screened applications for credit cards and insurance. You can opt-out for five years or opt-out permanently. If you change your mind, you can always opt-in to receive these offers on the same website.

Urban Legend Number 2: PRE-APPROVED CREDIT CARD
APPLICATIONS INDICATE I HAVE GOOD CREDIT.

Plastic Reactions:

- What positive emotions did you feel when you
  received the credit card application with the pre-
  approved status?
- What would cause you to apply for a new credit
  card based on a pre-approved status?
- Were you relieved to get a pre-approved
  application because your cash flow was tight?
- Were you considering using this credit card for
  use with everyday living expenses?
- Were you surprised to get the offer because you
  were afraid to look at your current credit score?
- What negative emotions would be triggered, if
  any, if you sent in the pre-approved application
  and you did not receive the credit card?
- How would such a denial make you feel?

URBAN LEGEND – 3

Not activating a new credit card has no effect.

Urban Legend Number 3: I applied for and received a new credit card. However, I have changed my mind about using it, and I never called the credit card company to activate it. Therefore, the credit card company will not report the new card to the credit bureaus, and my credit score will not be affected.

The Reality: _False_.

When you apply for a credit card, the credit card company makes a _hard inquiry_ on your credit report and your credit score will go down, as was discussed in **Urban Legend 1.**

In addition, if you are approved to receive the credit card, the approval will be reported by the credit card company to the three credit bureaus.

A new entry will appear on your credit report indicating you have another credit card with its associated credit limit. The new credit card will add an additional amount of credit that will be considered when your _credit utilization_ is analyzed (See **Urban Legend 7**).

The new entry will be created within a few days after the notice of your approval is received by the credit bureaus from the credit card company, even if the card is never activated.

Polly's Pearls of Wisdom: Only apply for a new credit card if you actually intend to use it.

All applications for new credit cards result in *hard inquiries* that lower your credit score.

If you change your mind after you apply for a new credit card, call the credit card company immediately, and try to have the card canceled before the *hard inquiry* credit check is initiated.

If you receive a new credit card and decide not to use it, you should consider calling the credit card company to activate it anyway, for at least two reasons.

First, an un-activated card can be easily forgotten, lost, or stolen, and may be used for fraudulent purchases.

Activity on an activated credit card can be monitored by routinely viewing your own credit card statements and your own credit report.

Your personal liability for unauthorized credit card charges on an activated credit card is limited to only $50.00 if the fraud is reported. In most instances, the credit card issuers routinely waive the $50.00 (see **Urban Legend 21**).

The credit card companies also routinely monitor activated credit cards for suspicious activity to prevent fraudulent purchases.

The credit bureaus, the credit card companies, and other business organizations offer credit monitoring services, identity theft monitoring, and identity theft insurance (see **Urban Legend 4**).

Second, credit cards with low interest rates, extra miles or points, or cash credits require activation and use to receive the benefit of the desired offerings.

Urban Legend Number 3: NOT ACTIVATING A NEW CREDIT CARD HAS NO EFFECT.

One negative for activating a credit card you are not going to use is that once your card is activated, you have accepted the contract terms associated with the credit card, including any annual fee. Even if you never activate the card, the amount of available credit for this card is added into your total available credit that is considered when you apply for a major purchase (e.g., mortgage or automobile loan).

Plastic Reactions:

- What positive or negative emotional triggers caused you to apply for the new credit card in the first place?
- What feelings or emotions may have caused you to change your mind about activating the new credit card?

URBAN LEGEND – 4

Not signing a credit
card has no effect.

Urban Legend Number 4: I have just received a new credit card in the mail. Instead of my signature, I always write "Ask for ID," "Check ID," "See ID," or something similar. This prevents fraudulent use of my credit card, because a store clerk must verify my identity before allowing a purchase on my credit card.

The Reality: _False_.

A credit card signed with anything other than your signature is invalid by the terms of your agreement with the credit card company.

One of the purposes of signing your credit card is to accept the contract terms you have with the credit card company that provided you with the credit card.

If you have signed your credit card with "Ask for ID," "Check ID," "See ID," "Compare Signatures," or something similar, the store clerk has the option to not accept the card for a transaction until it is properly signed. The merchant takes the liability for fraudulent transactions on an unsigned credit card.

A store clerk may actually require you sign the credit card with your full signature before the card can be used for a purchase. If you refuse to sign the credit card in front of the store clerk, your purchase may be refused because the credit card is invalid.

If a merchant accepts an unsigned credit card, the merchant risks financial liability if the purchaser later disputes the charges for that purchase.

Also, do not assume any merchant will ask you for additional identification when your credit card is used. A merchant is <u>not</u> obligated to ask for any identification at all before allowing use of a valid credit card that is signed. Many merchants do have their own security policies regarding this issue.

In fact, the merchant handbooks provided by many major credit card companies clearly state that a credit card sale <u>cannot</u> be conditioned on a purchaser providing additional identification when a valid credit card (i.e., properly signed) is presented.

**Polly's Pearls of Wisdom:** As a consumer, you are protected by law from any fraudulent use of your credit card. Because of this law, using anything other than your signature on your credit card really does nothing useful at all.

Many people do not sign their credit card because they are concerned that a thief will counterfeit the cardholder's signature. Fraud liability falls on the issuing bank and ultimately on the merchant who initiated a fraudulent transaction.

Abide by cardholder guidelines: sign your card when you receive it, activate it in a timely manner, monitor your monthly statements, and notify your bank if suspicious activity takes place.

A request for identification may not always work to prevent credit card fraud. If your credit card has been lost or stolen, there is a good chance other pieces of your identification have been lost or stolen as well (e.g., your wallet or purse was also stolen).

If your credit card has "Ask For ID" on the back and the store clerk asks for a signature, the thief may simply sign it with his/her own fraudulent signature in front of the store clerk.

A thief may also present both your stolen credit card and other stolen pieces of identification (i.e., typically identification without pictures) to fraudulently use the credit card for purchases.

One suggestion if you are worried about identity theft is to include both *your signature* on the card and "Ask for ID" or similar verbiage on the card. The advantage of this approach is that if a signature is required for a credit card transaction, a thief's signature on the credit card slip may not match your signature on the back of the credit card — that is, if the merchant actually takes the time to compare them!

The credit reporting bureaus, credit card companies, and other business organizations offer credit monitoring services, identity theft monitoring, and identity theft insurance.

All three credit reporting bureaus and other companies can provide credit monitoring services for a monthly fee. The three major credit bureaus also offer additional services, such as access to your credit reports, credit scores, and identity theft protection. You can find these services at:

Equifax (www.equifax.com/credit-watch-gold/),
Experian (www.experian.com/consumer-
products/credit-monitoring.html) and TransUnion
(www.transunion.com/personal-credit/credit-
management/credit-monitoring.page).

Such credit monitoring services send you a paper
letter, e-mail, or text message (depending on your
preferences) if there are any new inquiries to your credit
reports. However, many types of identity theft actions
are not detected by such credit monitoring services.

The credit monitoring services typically cost $10-
$25 per month, or $120-$300 per year. Many consumer
advocates question whether the cost is worth the money
paid for the type of actual protection received.

One of the problems with credit monitoring
services is that you may not receive any notification until
a negative entry is actually added to your credit report.
At the point a negative entry appears on your credit
report, a nefarious act has already taken place. It is
typically more difficult, time consuming, and expensive
to try to fix an identity theft problem at that point than if
you had been able to detect it before it was reported to
the credit bureaus.

One advantage of identity theft monitoring
services is that they alert you to identity theft at the point
someone else is trying to use your information to apply
for a new credit card, mortgage, or loan. It is typically
much easier to prevent identity theft before it happens
rather than remove it after it happens.

Urban Legend Number 4: NOT SIGNING A CREDIT CARD HAS NO EFFECT.

Popular identity theft monitoring services include Life Lock (www.lifelock.com), Identity Guard (www.identityguard.com) and Trusted ID (www.trustedid.com). A company called Identity Theft Labs (www.identitytheftlabs.com) currently provides a comparison of the features of popular identity theft services, including those listed.

Plastic Reactions:

- Ask yourself why you do not want to sign your credit card. Are you concerned that if you sign your credit card, and that card is stolen, it will lead to identity theft?
- Knowing you have no liability for fraudulent transactions on your credit card, what actions could you take to make you feel secure?

URBAN LEGEND – 5

Making a late payment on one of my credit cards affects the interest rates on all of my credit cards.

Urban Legend Number 5: I paid one of my credit card bills late this month. My late payment allows the credit card issuers for all my other credit cards to automatically raise the interest rate on those cards even though I have never made a late payment on those cards.

The Reality: _False._

In the past, many credit card agreements included a _Universal Default clause_. The Universal Default clause allowed credit card issuers to enforce _default_ terms imposed on credit card holders who missed payments or exceeded their credit card limit with any credit card issuer.

The Universal Default clause allowed a credit card issuer to increase interest rates "at any time, for any reason." For example, if you paid your credit card bill late for your V-credit card, then the issuer for your V-credit card would report the late payment to the credit bureaus and it would be reflected on your credit report, where it could be seen by the issuers of your other credit cards. In the past, the credit card issuer for your M-credit card could automatically raise your interest rate on that card, even if you had never, ever, made a late payment on your M-credit card.

On May 22, 2009, President Barack Obama signed the Credit Card Accountability, Responsibility, and Disclosure Act (CARD Act) of 2009[4]. The bill went into effect on February 22, 2010, nine months after it was enacted.

The CARD Act of 2009 has effectively prevented credit card issuers from using Universal Default clauses in credit card agreements because the Act limits the ability of credit card issuers to raise interest rates on existing credit card balances.

Polly's Pearls of Wisdom: The impact of a *single* late payment on your credit score varies depending on your credit history.

A single 30-day late payment typically reduces a person's credit score by 60-110 points (ranging from 60-80 points if your credit score is in the 600s, to about 80-110 points if your credit score is in the 700s). A late payment typically remains on a person's credit report for seven years.

For more information on time limits for negative information on your credit report, see the Fair Credit Reporting Act (FCRA) online at: (www.ftc.gov/os/statutes/fcrajump.shtm).

Based on the CARD Act of 2009, credit card issuers can't increase interest rates on existing balances except in certain situations, including:

- You are more than sixty days late on a minimum payment for your credit card.
- Your credit card has a variable interest rate that your credit card issuer does not control. For example, your credit card interest rate may be the

"prime interest rate + 15.35 percent." The prime interest rate is an interest rate on short-term loans that banks charge their commercial customers. Your credit card issuer does not control the prime interest rate. If the prime interest rate was 3.25 percent, your credit card interest rate would be 18.60 percent (3.25% + 15.35%).

- A promotional interest rate has expired on your credit card. For example, your credit card issuer offered zero percent interest on all credit card balances for a six month period.
- A *credit card hardship program* you have been participating in has expired.

Many credit card issuers offer *credit card hardship programs* to cardholders. Such programs are offered because, in many instances, the credit card issuers would rather work with you for a specified time period instead of having you declare bankruptcy or default on what you owe. During the specified time period (e.g., one year), the credit card issuer may take actions such as temporarily reducing the interest rate you are paying or suspending all finance charges.

Be aware that credit card companies are in the business of making money. They focus their hardship programs to get you back to a place where you may be able to make normal payments on your credit card balance again.

In addition, if the credit card hardship program does cancel any of your credit card debt, you will receive an IRS Form 1099-C and the canceled debt will be considered additional income (See **Urban Legend 6**).

Plastic Reactions:

- What caused you to make a late payment?
- What negative emotions were triggered after you made the late payment?
- Can you forgive yourself for the late payment and move forward in a positive manner?

Urban Legend Number 5: MAKING A LATE PAYMENT ON ONE OF MY CREDIT CARDS AFFECTS THE INTEREST RATES ON ALL OF MY CREDIT CARDS.

URBAN LEGEND – 6

Credit card debt forgiveness has no tax consequences.

Urban Legend Number 6: I had trouble paying off my credit card balances. I was able to negotiate with my credit card company to have three-quarters of my current credit card debt forgiven in exchange for paying off the remaining balance in a timely manner. The credit card company has issued me an IRS Form 1099-C which indicates my forgiven debt is considered additional income. I should just ignore and discard the form since the matter is settled, and my forgiven debt cannot be considered additional income.

The Reality: *False.*

You should <u>never</u> ignore any communication you receive from the Internal Revenue Service (IRS). Any time you receive such a form from the IRS, you should consult your tax professional immediately.

The IRS Form 1099-C is a *Cancelation of Debt* form required by the IRS when debt is forgiven or canceled. Any lender who agrees to accept at least $600 less than the original credit card balance has to file an IRS Form 1099-C with the IRS. Under current tax laws of the United States, the IRS considers canceled or forgiven debt as *additional income* that is subject to income taxes and must be reported.

The IRS considers canceled debt as additional income because you have received the monetary value of the forgiven debt, even if the majority of the balance was compounded interest and late fees charged by the bank.

If you ignore the IRS Form 1099-C you receive, you are at increased risk for IRS fines, tax penalties, interest penalties, audits, or even criminal penalties.

The IRS Form 1099-C is issued by creditors such as financial institutions, credit unions, the US government, the US Postal Service, the US Military, and other organizations "having a significant trade or business of lending money."

Suppose your outstanding credit card balance was $20,000 and you negotiated with your credit card company to forgive 75 percent of the debt (i.e., $15,000). You agree to pay off the remaining $5,000 in a timely manner. The credit card company then issues you an IRS Form 1099-C for the $15,000 amount of canceled debt. The $15,000 of forgiven debt is considered to be $15,000 of additional income on which you <u>must</u> pay taxes. The amount of taxes you have to pay is dependent upon your tax bracket.

Always consult your tax professional to determine the appropriate procedures to properly deal with the IRS Form 1099-C and to identify potential use of the IRS Form 982 exceptions.

Polly's Pearls of Wisdom: Sorry Virginia, there is no such thing as a free lunch or *free* debt forgiveness.

I know how you must feel about this…you're probably thinking, "How can the majority of my debt (which was mostly late fees, overlimit fees, bank fees,

Urban Legend Number 6: CREDIT CARD DEBT FOREGIVENESS HAS NO TAX CONSEQUENCES.

and large amounts of interest charged by the bank) be considered income to me when the debt is forgiven, and why is it taxable?" You might consider challenging this with your state government officials. This act alone may help you feel more in control of your credit health.

Before trying to negotiate cancellation of any credit card debt, consult with your tax professional and your financial planning professional.

Ask at least the following questions:

- What is my tax impact?
- Would it be better for me to pay a private company and not cancel any debt, or to cancel debt and be responsible for paying additional taxes to the IRS?

When you ask about your tax impact, ask what your tax impact will be for different scenarios of debt cancelation.

For example, you should ask your tax professional, "What are the tax consequences for me negotiating cancelation of 10 percent, 20 percent, or 30 percent of my credit card debt?"

This will help you determine if you can actually afford to pay the taxes on the additional income you must report as a result of having some portion of your debt canceled.

The impact of debt cancellation on your credit score varies depending on your credit history. Any debt cancellation typically reduces a person's credit score by 45-125 points (45-65 points if your credit score is in the 600s, and about 100-125 points if your credit score is in the 700s). Any debt cancellation typically remains on your credit report for seven years.

Please be aware that credit card companies, financial institutions, and other debt settlement companies are under no obligation to inform you of the tax consequences of setting any debt and typically will not do so.

There are currently no U.S. laws that require any company forgiving debt to disclose that the company will be issuing an IRS Form 1099-C to both the IRS and the consumer when any debt is forgiven.

However, many financial institutions now routinely include at least a minimal disclosure that an IRS Form 1099-C will be issued for all debt forgiveness settlements. However, no additional details are usually provided.

The IRS is a government organization that can impose *criminal penalties* on you for delinquent taxes and you may possibly be sent to jail if you are convicted. The IRS can also file a tax lien on all your properties, or impose a levy on all your bank accounts — freezing all your funds. When the IRS takes such actions, you typically have a very short time period (e.g., twenty-one days) to hire an attorney and respond to the allegations. Obviously, these actions can have serious repercussions that will affect your ability to pay your bills and will affect your credit score.

Urban Legend Number 6: CREDIT CARD DEBT FOREGIVENESS HAS NO TAX CONSEQUENCES.

A private company can initiate litigation and possibly obtain a civil legal judgment against you for non-payment of your outstanding debt. Enforcement of the judgment can include garnishment of your wages. Such a legal judgment will be reported to the three credit bureaus and will lower your credit score.

If you cannot pay your credit cards, would you rather pay a private company, which in a worst-case scenario can impose financial penalties via the civil legal system; or the IRS, which in a worst-case scenario could impose criminal penalties on you? Remember, you can avoid the worst-case scenario by paying your debt or your tax obligation in a timely fashion.

If you do decide to negotiate cancelation of your credit card debt, please make sure that you have done the following:

(1) Consulted with your tax professional so that you clearly understand your tax liabilities.

(2) Verified your current address with the creditor who is forgiving your credit card debt. The creditor will issue an IRS Form 1099-C and report it to the IRS with your current address on file with the creditor. If you have moved or are thinking about moving, you must report your current address to the creditor. The IRS does not accept as an excuse that you never received the Form 1099-C because the address on the form was incorrect or you have recently moved!

(3) When you receive the IRS Form 1099-C, check that the amount of debt forgiven is correct. If you see an error, contact the creditor forgiving the debt immediately

in writing via certified mail and request correction of the error by the creditor. Unfortunately, few creditors will issue a corrected Form 1099-C to the IRS. You must also contact the IRS about the error. You can use correspondence with the creditor to document your attempts to the correct the Form 1099-C error.

The IRS has clearly stated that the *"burden is placed on taxpayers"* to correct errors when any debt cancelation amounts on a Form 1099-C are incorrectly or inadequately reported by creditors or third-party debt collectors.

(4) Check that your monthly payment for the creditor has been reduced to reflect the amount of debt that was canceled. Do not make payments on debt that has been canceled, especially debt that you are going to have considered as additional income.

(5) Make sure the debt has actually been forgiven by the creditor before paying taxes to the IRS. You are not obligated to pay the IRS taxes on the debt until it is actually forgiven.

Many shady collection companies will actually issue a bogus Form 1099-C to debtors without ever canceling any credit card debt. They try to coerce the debtor to pay off their entire credit card debt because the IRS is supposedly involved and the IRS can put you in jail. So be diligent when you receive an IRS Form 1099-C.

More information on IRS Form 1099-C rules and the IRS Form 982 exceptions for the 1099-C are available online at: (www.irs.gov/instructions/i1099ac/index.html).

Urban Legend Number 6: CREDIT CARD DEBT FOREGIVENESS HAS NO TAX CONSEQUENCES.

Plastic Reactions:

- What steps can you take to address the issue of your credit card debt?
- How did you feel after a portion of your credit card debt was forgiven?
- Were you aware that your forgiven debt was subject to taxes?
- Until you read this chapter did you even know what an IRS Form 1099-C was? Most people have no idea!

URBAN LEGEND – 7

Paying off my credit card balances in full every month will never affect my credit score.

Urban Legend Number 7: I use my credit cards instead of cash to make purchases every month. I pay all my credit cards in full at the end of each month. My credit score will never go down if I pay my balance in full at the end of each month.

The Reality: _False._

The credit card bureaus do not care if you pay off your credit cards in full each month.

One of the factors that determine your credit score is your _credit utilization_. This factor accounts for 30 percent of your total credit score.

Your _credit utilization_ is a ratio of your credit card balances to available credit limits as listed on your credit report. For example, if your credit limit for all your credit cards totals is $20,000 and you have an $11,000 credit card balance this month, your credit utilization is 55 percent ($11,000/$20,000 x 100).

The lower your credit utilization is, the higher this portion of your credit score will be, because a lower percentage indicates you are using a smaller amount of the credit you have available to you.

If you exceed certain limits on your credit utilization, your credit score can actually go down, even if you pay your balance in full at the end of every month.

Why does this happen? Unless you pay your bill before the due date, the credit card bureaus will not see a zero balance for your account. Your outstanding balance will contribute to your credit utilization, even though you pay the balance in full.

Credit utilization scores are calculated in two parts, using two different calculations. If your credit utilization score for either part exceeds a pre-determined threshold, your credit score will go down.

Any credit utilization score above approximately 15 percent will cause your credit score to decline by about 3-5 points.

First, an *individual credit utilization* score is calculated separately for each of your credit cards.

For example, if you have two credit cards and the first card has a limit of $1,200 and you have a balance of $450, your credit utilization is 37.5 percent for the first card. If your second card has a credit limit of $1,500 and you have a balance of $1,350, your credit utilization is 90 percent. Since the credit utilization values for each of these cards is above 15 percent, your credit score will go down. Even if the credit utilization value was below 15 percent for one of the cards, your credit score would still be negatively impacted.

Second, an *aggregate credit utilization* score is calculated for your total balance on all your credit cards against your total credit limits for all cards. Continuing the example, you have a total credit limit of $2,700 ($1,200 + $1,500) and a total credit card balance of $1,800 ($450 + $1,350). Your credit utilization score is 66 percent ($1,800/$2,700 x 100). This is also a high number, so your credit score will go down.

In this example, the calculated credit utilization scores for both sections of the test have exceeded the pre-determined threshold. However, your credit score will only go down once and not twice.

Polly's Pearls of Wisdom: The impact of *credit utilization* on your credit score varies depending on your credit history.

Credit utilization typically reduces a person's credit score by 0-15 points based on credit utilization scores (0-15 percent = zero points), (~16-29 percent = 3 point reduction), (~30-50 percent = 5 point reduction), (~51-64 percent = 7 point reduction) and (> 65 percent = 15 point reduction).

To keep your credit score high, keep your credit utilization scores low.

If you have a month in which you need to make a big purchase that causes you to have a high credit utilization ratio, and your credit score goes down, pay off your balance and keep your credit utilization low (e.g., < 15 percent) for about the next 6-9 months. Your credit score will rebound over time.

If you find yourself in this situation, you can also pay off your balance early (i.e., before the due date), and before the end of the month. Most credit card companies report payment information only once a month at the end of each month. If you pay your credit card balance in full, early, and before the end of the month (when your credit card company will report your on-time payment of your whole balance to the credit bureaus), your account will have a balance of zero at the end of the month, and you will have a very good credit utilization for this account.

Another way to ensure that you always have the lowest credit utilization is to make multiple payments throughout the month.

There are several advantages of paying your credit cards off in full every month. You are able to use the credit card company's money interest-free each month. You also avoid amassing a large amount of credit card debt. In addition, your credit utilization could remain low, depending on how you use your credit cards. Finally, you are establishing and maintaining a positive payment history over a long period of time.

However, also be careful when making all your purchases with credit cards instead of cash. A sudden job loss, a death, a medical emergency, a significant family problem, or some other unexpected emergency may leave you unable to pay off your credit card balances in full. Such events could force you to make a late payment, which can cause your credit score to drop by 50-100 points.

If want to continue to use your credit cards for all your purchases, set up a reserve savings fund that always has enough money to pay off your average monthly credit card balances in the event of any emergency.

Urban Legend Number 7: PAYING OFF MY CREDIT CARD BALANCES
IN FULL EVERY MONTH WILL NEVER AFFECT MY CREDIT SCORE.

Plastic Reactions:

- How important is your credit score to you?
- Do you use your credit score to define a part of your self-esteem?
- Do you compare yourself to others with your credit score?
- How frequently do you check your credit score?
- Do you have an emergency savings fund to help you with credit card debt if a life event beyond your control (e.g., a job loss or a death in your family) changed your financial circumstances?

URBAN LEGEND – 8

A credit card issuer must accept my payment no matter what the amount is.

Urban Legend Number 8: I have a large credit card balance I am having trouble paying off. I can decide what minimum payment I can afford and send in that amount instead. The credit card company must accept my own minimum payment.

The Reality: *False.*

You are obligated under the terms of the credit card agreement to make the designated minimum payment each month. You cannot decide to change your minimum payment and send in a different payment amount instead.

Your credit card issuer will likely accept your payment, even if it is not the minimum payment. Your payment will always be accepted because payments are processed at large payment processing centers without scrutiny or review during payment data input.

If you don't pay the minimum payment, your credit card issuer may automatically charge you a late fee, raise your interest rate, and report the late payment to the credit bureaus. Your large credit card balance will increase and get larger every month.

Under the CARD Act of 2009, a credit card issuer is generally prohibited[5] from raising your interest rates unless you are more than sixty days late making your minimum payment.

If your interest rate is raised because you are more than sixty days late on your minimum payment, you are required to receive written notice from your credit card issuer.

If you pay at least your minimum payment on time for a six-month period, you can request that your credit card issuer review your account. They may agree to lower your interest rate.

**Polly's Pearls of Wisdom:** If you cannot make your minimum payment, call your credit card issuer and ask what options are available to you.

If you have a good payment history and you can convince your credit card issuer that this is a one-time occurrence, your credit card issuer may extend your due date for the payment, waive the late fee, and not report your non-payment or late payment to the credit bureaus.

However, there is no requirement that your credit card issuer offer you such courtesies if you miss your minimum payment. In addition, even if your credit card issuer did allow you to not make a minimum payment, they are not likely to allow you do that more than once.

If you are in a position where you cannot make your minimum payments, you should consider seeking credit counseling to assist you in managing your finances.

A good reference for credit counseling is the
National Foundation for Credit Counseling (NFCC). The
NFCC is a non-profit agency with credit counseling
experts who are specifically trained to help you reduce
your debt. For more information on credit counseling
visit (www.nfcc.org) or call (800)388-2227 (see **Urban
Legend 24**).

Plastic Reactions:

- What emotions are you feeling as a result of not
  being able to make a minimum payment on your
  credit card?
- Realizing that your credit score will drop a large
  number of points from missing a payment can
  cause additional worry or anxiety. Describe that
  emotion here.
- Do you think you can benefit from credit
  counseling?

URBAN LEGEND – 9

Canceling a credit card will not affect my credit score.

Urban Legend Number 9: I just moved my entire outstanding credit card balance from my old credit card to a new credit card with a zero percent interest rate for six months. I am going to cancel my old credit card and another credit card with a zero balance that I no longer use. I will only have the new credit card after the balance transfer. Canceling my two credit cards will not affect my credit score.

The Reality: *False.*

Your credit score will fall because of several factors. First, it is likely that your *credit utilization* (30 percent of your credit score) will change when two credit cards are canceled (see **Urban Legend 7**). Also, applying for the new credit card will cause a *hard inquiry* to be generated by the new credit card issuer (see **Urban Legend 1**). Additionally, since you canceled two cards with a credit history over some period, and all you have left is a brand new card with no credit history, the length of your credit history will change.

By canceling two of your credit cards, you are eliminating a large amount of your available credit. As a result, you are significantly increasing your credit utilization values.

For example, suppose your old credit card had a $5,000 limit and you had a $1,400 balance on it. You transfer the $1,400 balance to the new credit card which has a $3,000 limit. Your other ten-year-old credit card has a zero balance and a $4,000 limit. You then cancel the both of your older credit cards.

Your *individual credit utilization* before the transfer would be 28 percent ($1,400/$5,000 x 100) for the first old card and zero percent ($0/$4,000 x 100) for the other old card. Your *aggregate credit utilization* would be 15.5 percent ($1,400/($5,000 + $4,000) x 100). Before the balance transfer, the credit utilization ratios are pretty good.

After the balance transfer, since you only have one credit card remaining, your *individual and aggregate credit utilization ratios* would both be 46.6 percent ($1,400/$3,000 x 100). As can be clearly seen, canceling two of your credit cards has significantly increased your credit utilization values. This will lower your credit score.

Thirty-five percent of your credit score is based on your *credit utilization*. As was discussed in **Urban Legend 7**, a higher credit utilization value is likely to lower your credit score.

Ten percent of your credit score is based on *credit inquiries*. As was discussed in **Urban Legend 1**, a *hard inquiry* is likely to lower your credit score.

Fifteen percent of your credit score is based on the *age of credit accounts*. Decreasing the ages of your credit accounts by opening new accounts and closing old accounts is likely to lower your credit score.

Polly's Pearls of Wisdom: The exact impact of opening and closing credit card accounts on your credit score will vary depending on your credit history.

However, when three factors which account for 60 percent of your total credit score are involved, you should expect your credit score to fall by 5-10 points or more.

Before you open a new credit card account, you should consider asking the bank where you have a long-term credit card relationship to match the new bank's offer. If you have a good payment record with the older card, they may do so. Remember, older cards with a long payment record have a positive impact on your credit score.

You should also consider that the bank offering you the new credit card has no relationship with you and no historical data on you. Therefore, they may assume you are only interested in this good introductory offer and that you will not become a long-time customer. They may be less likely to work with you if you encounter financial hardship than a bank with which you have maintained a long-term relationship.

Doing a balance transfer to the new credit card with a zero percent interest rate for six months may save you a significant amount of money each month. To fully take advantage of such a credit card, make every effort to completely pay off your credit card by the end of the six month period.

Also, read the fine print to understand what the zero percent interest annual percentage rate (APR) actually covers. Will the zero percent card cover only your old credit card debt that you transferred, or will it also cover new purchases? Does it have a higher annual fee than your current credit card? Does it change the rewards you receive (e.g., airline miles or points)? Will the "normal" interest rate after the zero percent interest period actually be a higher percentage than your old credit card?

Many times an interest rate on many zero percent balance transfer cards may also automatically go from zero percent to a very high percentage in the event of any late or missed payments.

As was discussed previously, there are a number of websites that allow you to compare credit card offers, including those that offer zero percent interest for balance transfers and for new purchases. See **Urban Legend 2** for details.

Plastic Reactions:

- Why would you want to close a long-time lending relationship?
- Did you consider asking the loyal long-term bank to meet the new bank's offer?
- What were you feeling about leaving a long-term credit card partner? They may have been with you since college.

Urban Legend Number 9: CANCELING A CREDIT CARD WILL NOT AFFECT MY CREDIT SCORE.

URBAN LEGEND – 10

Exceeding my credit card limit does not affect my credit score.

Urban Legend Number 10: I have one credit card with a $300 limit. I have a $120 dollar balance on the card because I just went grocery shopping for the month for my family and I bought a lot of fresh and frozen food. My refrigerator broke down and cannot be repaired. I had to go to my local appliance store and purchase a refrigerator for $500 to save all my food from spoiling. I exceeded my credit limit on the card. Since the credit card company authorized the sale at the appliance store, I will not be charged any additional fees and my credit score will not be affected.

The Reality: *False*.

In this situation, a credit card issuer can take several actions: decline the transaction; accept the transaction and charge an over-limit fee; or even increase your interest rate for going over your limit by a large amount.

If you have an *excellent* credit score, the credit card issuer may automatically raise your credit limit and accept the transaction without charging you any additional fees. However, such a scenario is usually reserved for credit scores of 800+.

Since the transaction was approved by the credit card issuer, you will likely be charged an over-limit fee of $25-$35. The exact amount depends on your credit card agreement. Under the CARD Act, you must *opt-in* to allow over-limit purchases and to accept over-limit fees. If you do not opt-in for over-limit transactions, most likely you will be declined for the transaction. Note that your minimum payment will increase immediately.

Be aware that the over-limit fee is typically due immediately, and if you do not pay the fee immediately, a late fee charge may be added during the next billing cycle. Under new rules imposed by the CARD Act, banks can no longer charge you more than one penalty fee per billing cycle (i.e., a late fee, an over-limit fee, or a non-sufficient funds fee, etc.).

The credit card issuers may also increase your interest to a higher rate based on the over-limit scenario. In addition, an over-limit charge may also push your *default* interest rate to a higher level. Again, the exact actions taken by your credit card issuer depends on the terms of your credit card agreement.

Your credit score will go down because, when you exceed your credit limit, you have maxed-out your credit card, and your *credit utilization* is actually <u>over</u> 100 percent because you are using all of your available credit and more. Remember, your credit utilization accounts for 30 percent of your credit score.

Polly's Pearls of Wisdom: You may be amazed at the amount of revenue that late fees generate for the credit card companies. The CARD Act of 2009 has helped to reduce that amount, but it is still an enormous sum. Prior to the implementation of the CARD Act, Americans paid almost $15 billion in penalty fees per year[6].

Urban Legend 10: EXCEEDING MY CREDIT CARD LIMIT DOES NOT AFFECT MY CREDIT SCORE.

According to the *"CARD Act Factsheet"* published by the Consumer Finance Protection Bureau in February 2011, the total amount of late fees paid by American consumers dropped by almost half in the first year after the CARD Act was enacted, from $901 million in January 2010 (before the CARD Act late fee rules went into effect) to $427 million in November 2010 (after the CARD Act was implemented)[7]. Note that these amounts are per <u>month</u>. Obviously, penalty fees are still a huge source of revenue for the credit card companies.

You need to be aware that a maxed-out credit card will cause your credit score to go down by 10-40 points (about 10-20 points for a credit score in the 600s, and about 20-40 points for a credit score in the 700s).

If you find yourself in such an emergency situation, what should you do? One of the easiest things to do would be to call your credit card issuer *before* you make the purchase, explain the situation, and ask them to raise your credit limit. If you are a good customer, the credit card issuer is likely to raise your limit and allow you to make the emergency purchase.

If you have opted-in to allow over-limit purchases and you cannot call your credit card issuer *before* you made the over-limit purchase, call your credit card issuer immediately after the purchase and explain the emergency situation.

If this over limit event is a one-time, isolated event, your credit card issuer may waive the over-limit fees, and/or not change the interest rate you are paying or raise your default interest rate.

Remember, the credit card issuer is <u>not</u> obligated to waive any fees or not adjust any interest rates. However, they may do so as a courtesy to you in certain circumstances.

Aside from the emergency event used in the Urban Legend example, how can you ensure that you stay below your credit limit?

- Invest in a small notebook and write down every purchase you make. Keep a running total of what you spend each month on your credit cards. When you see that you are within 12 percent of your credit limit, stop using that credit card. Make a note in your book of what that amount is for easy reference.
- Try to keep your credit card balances low. The advantage to this is if you have an emergency, then you will have the available credit to handle the problem.
- A tool that can help you manage your outstanding balances is a service offered by your credit card bank. They will send you an email or text alert notifying you when you are getting close to your credit limit. Many banks provide this service for free.

Remember, the CARD Act of 2009 does not allow your credit card issuer to charge you over-limit fees unless you agree to *opt-in* to pay such fees. If you decide not to opt-in, then an over-limit transaction will be declined at the point of sale and you will not be charged any fees or interest penalties. In 2010, the percentage of accounts charged over-limit fees dropped from 12 percent down to 1 percent because of the opt-in requirement for over-limit fees[8]. You can decide to not allow yourself to be caught in this predicament by not opting-in to over-limit charges and by planning for emergencies.

Plastic Reactions:

- How do you typically react to a financial or personal emergency situation? Can you think clearly, decide what to do, and take the proper action steps?
- What type of financial or personal emergency plan could you have in place for the future?

URBAN LEGEND – 11

My credit card with a radio chip for speed paying is not vulnerable to electronic fraud.

Urban Legend Number 11: My credit card has a Radio Frequency Identifier (RFID) chip. I use this credit card for making speedy purchases at restaurants and gas stations by passing the card by a card reader. My credit card is not vulnerable to electronic fraud since it has the RFID chip.

The Reality: _False._

About one-third of all credit cards issued by credit card issuers in the United States already have an RFID chip included in them. These credit cards are called *smart cards, swipe-and-go cards,* or *tap-and-go cards.* However, many smart cards have more hardware (e.g., a microprocessor or memory) than just an RFID chip. The RFID chip continuously transmits a radio signal from your credit card. The radio signal typically includes at least your credit card number and its expiration date in an unsecure (i.e., not encrypted) format. Several credit card issuers have indicated that they are considering encrypting RFID signals on credit cards to help to prevent fraud.

Swipe-and-go credit cards are used to make a purchase by holding the card about four inches from an RFID reader on a Point of Sale (POS) device at a merchant location. It has been estimated that using such swipe-and-go cards cuts the time required to make a credit card purchase from a few minutes down to just a few seconds.

The credit card issuers claim the swipe-and-go cards are more secure than regular credit cards because the RFID signal is unique to your credit card and uniquely identifies you; and each time an RFID purchase transaction is completed, the RFID chip generates a unique transaction code, specifically and only for the transaction. This transaction code is used in a similar way that a security code is used on a conventional credit card when it is processed.

However, the RFID signal can be easily intercepted by an $8 RFID signal reader that anyone can buy at a local electronics retailer or on the Internet. If your RFID signal is intercepted, your credit card can be used for one fraudulent transaction of any amount.

If the RFID signal from your credit card is stolen, it presents a situation similar to that of having your credit card number stolen, even though you are still in possession of the card. If your RFID signal is stolen, you are usually not liable for any fraudulent purchases made with your stolen credit card number (see **Urban Legend 21**).

Since the RFID chip is transmitting a signal that is not stopped by a typical purse or wallet, a thief with an $8 RFID signal reader can obtain your credit card information from the RFID chip simply by walking by you. RFID thieves typically target RFID credit card holders in train stations, bus stations, airports, shopping malls, and on the street. So beware!

Polly's Pearls of Wisdom: So how can you tell if your credit card is a card with an RFID chip? Such credit cards usually have visual identifiers that indicate the credit card has an RFID chip. The visual identifiers include a series of curved lines resembling parentheses that go from smaller to larger (e.g.,)))).This symbol is used to illustrate the radio signal emitted by the RFID chip. The card may also include a trade name or trademark such as *PayPass*, *PayWave*, or *Blink* to indicate the card has an RFID chip.

You can also check the documentation you received with your credit card when it was mailed to you. If you cannot determine if your card has an RFID chip, just call your credit card issuer and ask.

If you do not want a credit card with an RFID chip, or do not or will not use the speed pay option of such a card, call your credit card issuer and ask for a credit card without the RFID chip.

RFID chips are becoming common in debit cards and ATM cards as well as credit cards, and RFID chips are being used on newer US passports.

Debit cards and ATM cards are subject to much different rules than credit cards with respect to fraudulent purchases. If your RFID signal is stolen from a debit card or ATM card, and you do not report your debit card or ATM card number stolen or do not report fraudulent purchases within a specified time frame, you could be subject to penalties of all the money in the accounts associated with your debit card (**See Urban Legend 21**). So if your debit card or ATM card has an RFID chip, be very, very careful when using it!

Many people who have credit cards with an RFID chip purchase an RFID blocking sleeve for the card. The RFID blocking sleeve is typically a plastic or plastic coated paper sleeve with RFID signal-blocking material on the inside of the sleeve.

If you want to protect your credit card with an RFID chip, there are a number of companies that sell RFID blocking sleeves, wallets and purses. You can purchase such products to protect your credit cards with RFID chips at Identity Stronghold (www.idstronghold.com), Tamper Seal (www.tamperseal.com) and other retailers.

If you do not want to purchase any products at all, a simple solution to protect your RFID credit card is to simply wrap it in a taped piece of aluminum foil. This will prevent anyone from intercepting the RFID signal from your credit card.

Plastic Reactions:

- Were you aware the credit cards had an RFID chip before reading this chapter?
- Is it beneficial to your credit health to make purchases faster and easier?

Urban Legend Number 11: MY CREDIT CARD WITH A RADIO CHIP FOR SPEED PAYING IS NOT VULNERABLE TO ELECTRONIC FRAUD.

- Will you tend to make purchases more often with this type of credit card?

URBAN LEGEND – 12

A divorce does not change my credit card obligations.

Urban Legend Number 12: I have just gotten divorced from my spouse. We had a credit card account that included both of our names. The account had a $1,000 balance. The divorce decree indicates my spouse was responsible for paying off the credit card. My spouse has stopped paying on the credit card. The credit card issuer is initiating collection actions against me. I am not responsible for paying off the credit card and my credit score will not be affected because of the divorce decree.

The Reality: *False.*

According to US Census data[9], the divorce rate for marriages in the United States has hovered around 50 percent for many years. Financial stress is commonly regarded as one of the "Top 10" reasons that people get divorced. Unfortunately, understanding what your credit card rights and obligations are during and after a divorce is something many of you will need to know.

You and your spouse entered into a contract with the credit card issuer while you were still married. If both of your names are on the credit card account, you are both liable for any outstanding balance — regardless of what your divorce decree may state. The divorce decree by itself does not change any such contracts with your credit card company.

A first option would be to try to get the credit card issuer to cancel the joint account, and have the credit card issuer to create an account for your spouse under his/her own name and transfer the credit card balance into that account. However, if the joint account has an outstanding balance with non-payment and collections actions, the credit card issuer is not likely to do so. You may also have a hard time getting your spouse to agree to do this.

If you are able to do so financially, the best solution would be to pay off the credit card in full and then request the joint account be canceled. In this situation, you would then have to take legal action against your spouse to recover the money that the divorce decree specified he/she pay on the credit card. You should consider whether or not you are ready to take more legal action against your spouse. It may cost more in attorney's fees to recover the money than what you spent to pay off the credit card.

You can also make a request to the collections agency to accept interest-only payments. This alternative will lower the required payment, and will allow you time to determine a permanent solution to the problem.

Another option is to contact your divorce attorney, explain the situation, and ask what can be done.

In the past, such situations were common due to the emotional issues associated with going through a divorce. However, in the last few years the dynamic has changed because of the state of the economy in the US and throughout the world. Many people have lost their jobs and have become unemployed for long periods of time. They are simply unable to pay their credit card bills, divorce decree or not.

Urban Legend Number 12: A DIVORCE DOES NOT CHANGE MY CREDIT CARD OBLIGATIONS.

Your credit score and the credit score of your spouse will both go down by a large number of points because of the non-payment on the account and the collections actions.

Polly's Pearls of Wisdom: The negative impact of divorce on your credit score will be directly related to your credit history, both before and during the divorce. Although this is a very emotional time, you should also focus on your long-term recovery, both financial and emotional. You should consider that, if you can afford to do so, paying off a credit card balance may save you money in the long run and it may benefit your financial well-being.

It is easy to be angry at your spouse for not paying a bill that a judge said they had to in the divorce decree, but if you pay off that bill, you can take back control of your finances and shorten the amount of time spent fighting with your spouse. Doing so will also help your mental and physical health by removing the stress of collections and other legal actions that will be taken against you for non-payment of a credit card account. Reducing the amount of time that you have negative items being reported on your credit report will shorten the time your credit score will need to recover.

As was discussed for **Urban Legend 5**, a single *missed payment* typically reduces a person's credit score by 60-110 points (about 60-80 points if your credit score is in the 600s, and about 80-110 points if your credit score is in the 700s). A missed payment entry typically remains on a person's credit report for seven years.

A *collection action* typically reduces a person's credit score by 40-160 points (about 60-80 points if your credit score is in the 600s, and about 140-160 points if your credit score is in the 700s) and remains on a person's credit report for seven years.

It is best to try and handle responsibility for credit card issues during the divorce proceedings. Divorce laws vary from state-to-state and you must consult with your divorce attorney to discuss such issues.

If an agreement can be reached during the divorce proceedings as to which spouse will be responsible for what portion of the credit card debt, then you can have your attorney contact the credit card issuer and request the joint account be canceled. Ask the credit card issuer to open new accounts for both you and your spouse individually, and to issue you a new credit card on your new individual account. The debt on these new accounts will not be shared, and you can move forward from that point.

If an agreement cannot be reached during the divorce proceedings, immediately upon receiving your divorce decree you should contact the credit card company in writing and request the joint account be canceled, and new individual accounts be set up for you and your former spouse. Include a copy of the divorce decree with your letter.

Urban Legend Number 12: A DIVORCE DOES NOT CHANGE MY
CREDIT CARD OBLIGATIONS.

Obtain copies of all three of your credit reports,
and continue to monitor your credit reports until all your
joint accounts can be canceled. This will alert you to any
problems that are occurring (e.g., late payments, missed
payments, or collections actions).

Be aware that the new credit card accounts you
and your spouse obtain may have different contract
terms, new credit limits, and different interest rates.
Because your financial situation has changed, you both
may be required to reapply with the issuing bank. The
credit cards for the joint account were issued based on
combined incomes. The credit cards for the individual
accounts will be issued for each spouse individually.

In many marriages (especially in those involving
older couples), one spouse may not have worked for
decades, and may have no job and no income after the
divorce. It may not seem fair, but in such a situation, the
non-working spouse may be issued a credit card with a
very low limit or even be denied a credit card altogether.
Ladies and gentlemen, as a rule of thumb, always, always,
always have a credit card in your own name.

The same thing may be true with mortgages and
auto loans. The non-working spouse or the spouse with
the smaller income simply may not make enough money
to qualify for such loans, or to refinance such loans.

More information about your credit card rights
after a divorce decree has been issued can be found the
Federal Trade Commission's website at:
(www.ftc.gov/bcp/edu/pubs/consumer/credit/cre08.shtm)

or by calling (877) FTC-HELP.

More information on divorce topics including your financial obligations during and after a divorce can be found online at: (www.divorcesupport.com) or (www.divorce360.com). Many other websites can be easily found using a search engine query on this topic.

A divorce is a very emotional situation. Anyone who has gone through a divorce knows that it generates a large number of emotions, both positive and negative. Be aware of the associated negative emotional triggers when making purchases of any kind. Consider the following.

<u>Plastic Reactions:</u>

- Loss of a marriage, a job or a change of residence caused by divorce can trigger grief emotions. Ask yourself, "Am I grieving? How do I feel?" See **Urban Legend 18** for a discussion on the stages of grief and where to get help with grief.
- How did you feel when you were dealing with closing your joint accounts?
- How would you feel if you had a new individual credit card account?
- How would you react if you were denied a new individual credit card account?

Urban Legend Number 12: A DIVORCE DOES NOT CHANGE MY
CREDIT CARD OBLIGATIONS.

URBAN LEGEND – 13

A credit card issuer can automatically garnish my bank account if I stop paying on my credit card.

Urban Legend Number 13: I have a large credit card balance and my minimum payment is over $1,000 per month. I lost my job and have not been able to find another. I am collecting unemployment, and my unemployment checks are deposited electronically into my bank account. I am living very simply. However, if I try to make payments on my credit card balance I do not have enough money to pay my rent and buy food for my kids. Since I have to survive, I just stopped making any payments at all on my credit card. The credit card company sent the matter to a collections agency. The collections agency can automatically garnish money from my bank account.

The Reality: _False_.

A creditor must file suit in the debtor's county and notify the individual of the impending lawsuit —giving him/her a chance to respond and defend him/herself.

If you are sued by a creditor, you should consult with an attorney immediately. If you cannot afford an attorney, at a minimum you should challenge the debt, and make sure the debt, the terms, and the amount of debt are accurate. Creditors can make mistakes and frequently do.

However, be aware if you challenge the debt in court and lose, you may have to pay court costs, fees, and maybe even attorney fees for the creditor's attorney.

For creditors other than credit card issuers, when you receive a notification of an outstanding debt and a request for payment, you should immediately send a letter via certified mail requesting a copy of all papers related to the ownership of the debt. In other words, make them prove that they actually own the debt and prove that you are actually the debtor.

It has become quite common for creditors to sell off old debts to collection agencies that are based outside the United States. Many of these old debts have been paid in full and the offshore collection agencies try to collect the debts again. This practice is creating a continual aggravation for a large number of debtors.

Each state has a statute of limitations in place to protect consumers from lawsuits over old debts between three and ten years old. The statute of limitations varies from state-to-state.

If the creditor wins a debt collection court case, the judge grants a judgment to the creditor. A certified court judgment is necessary to obtain a *writ of garnishment* for all creditors other than the federal government. *A writ of garnishment* is a court document indicating that the collection agency has the court's permission to seize funds.

A collection agency can periodically garnish your bank accounts until it recovers the full amount you owe. You can attempt to revoke the company's right to seize your accounts by appealing the court judgment that grants the collection agency its garnishment rights.

Although grounds for appeal vary, if the company failed to serve you with proper notice of the lawsuit that provided it with its right to garnish, or you do not owe the debt in question, you can file a motion with the court

Urban Legend Number 13: A CREDIT CARD ISSUER CAN AUTOMATICALLY GARNISH MY BANK ACCOUNT IF I STOP PAYING ON MY CREDIT CARD.

to have the collection agency's judgment vacated. If you succeed, the collection agency will lose its right to garnish your bank accounts.

A collection agency cannot garnish federal benefits such as Social Security payments, military annuities, student loans, survivor benefits, unemployment payments, retirement pensions, or public assistance payments.

Polly's Pearls of Wisdom: We all fully intend to be responsible and pay our bills on time, and when possible, pay them in full. With the current economy, many families have experienced a reduction in income. Receiving a legal action notice about a delinquent credit card account when you are under financial stress makes it even more difficult to find a solution that reduces the stress of being in debt.

A *legal collection action* or *delinquent account* typically reduces a person's credit score by 40-160 points (about 60-80 points if your credit score is in the 600s, and about 140-160 points if your credit score is in the 700s) and remains on a person's credit report for seven years.

A time period for any delinquent accounts starts approximately 180 days after a *date of first delinquency* on the account. The date of first delinquency is also known as the Fair Credit Reporting Act (FCRA) *Compliance Date*.

The statute of limitations is based on the date of first delinquency.

Consumers should be aware of a practice called *re-aging* of old debts. The clock on the statute of limitations for a legal collections action may start anew if a consumer makes a payment — even a small amount — on a credit card debt that has exceeded or is approaching the end of the statute of limitations.

Acknowledging an old debt may also extend the time limit on potential debt collection lawsuits. If you are the subject of a debt collection lawsuit, it is advisable to thoroughly discuss all your rights and options with an attorney.

Re-aging of a debt is a negative action taken by many creditors. The date of first delinquency is re-adjusted by a creditor to a later date.

Unscrupulous creditors have been known to intentionally reset a date of first delinquency to stretch out how long a derogatory account appears on a consumer's credit report as a penalty for having a delinquent account and to cause the consumer embarrassment.

However, such an act is illegal under the FCRA[10]. Violations of this provision of the FCRA may result in civil penalties for the creditor of $2,500 per violation.

Remember, a majority of credit reports include errors. Re-aging of a debt may not have been intentional, but simply an error. To correct a re-aging error on your credit report, you must contact the credit reporting bureaus and the creditors in writing as was discussed in the **What is a Credit Report?** section.

Re-aging of a debt can also be a positive action and can be requested by a consumer. A consumer may become delinquent on their debts only temporarily due to an emergency event. A consumer may request re-aging of their debt with a creditor in exchange for paying off the debt immediately or creating a payment plan.

If the creditor agrees, the consumer may enter into an agreement with a creditor to re-age the debt to prevent the debt from being reported as delinquent. This will prevent damage to a consumer's credit score and credit rating. However, not all creditors will agree to re-aging debt.

Also, remember to research any collections attempts taken against you. A common scam being perpetrated against consumers is when a collections agency attempts to collect on old debt or paid-off debt. This debt is referred to as "zombie debt." Zombie debt is typically old debt, often older than the statute of limitations which holds you legally responsible[11].

A creditor holding this debt will sell it to a collections agency, who will in turn sell this debt to another collections agency if collections actions are unsuccessful. The new collections agency will initiate additional collections actions against you. It is often difficult to determine where the debt originated on the statements sent by companies attempting to collect zombie debt. You may have even paid the debt off in the past, and the collections agency is attempting to collect it again.

When a collections agency contacts you, get their mailing address. You should send a certified letter requesting that they send you written documentation proving that the debt is valid. Further communications with the collections agency should be made only in writing via certified mail. Avoid talking with them on the telephone, as they may record the conversation and you will have no record of this conversation.

You should consult with an attorney to help you with the matter. If you make a payment on the debt, this will re-age the debt, and the statute of limitations will be reset for this debt. The statute of limitations for debt collection varies by state.

When you receive the documentation from the collections agency, check your records to see if this debt is actually yours or not. If you paid it off in the past, you can send a copy of the proof of payment via certified mail to the collections agent. Many times this will stop collections actions by one agency, but then they will re-sell the debt, causing your zombie debt to re-surface again and again.

You should check your credit report to see if this debt is being reported against you or not. If it is on your credit report, and this is an error, dispute the error on your credit report (see **What is a Credit Report?** for details on this process).

Urban Legend Number 13: A CREDIT CARD ISSUER CAN AUTOMATICALLY GARNISH MY BANK ACCOUNT IF I STOP PAYING ON MY CREDIT CARD.

You should also be aware that grief is a common emotion experienced when a person is going through job loss and the stressors associated with ensuing financial difficulties (see **Urban Legend 18** for details). Here are just a few of the organizations you could contact for support with these issues:

- **The American Counseling Association** – The ACA features a page on dealing with job loss, as well as other resources on their site. Their website: (www.counseling.org/Publications/).
- **University of Washington Human Resources** – The University of Washington offers a very informative website on layoff support resources. The page features a lengthy article about coping with job loss. Their website: (www.washington.edu/admin/hr/roles/ee/layoff/resources/coping.html).
- **Foreclosure Avoidance Counseling** – The Department of Housing and Urban Development (HUD) offers information and assistance in how to avoid foreclosure, if possible. HUD works with nonprofit agencies across the country to provide foreclosure counseling free of charge. Their website: (www.hud.gov/offices/hsg/sfh/hcc/fc/).

Plastic Reactions:

- What emotions did the loss of your job trigger?
- How did you feel when you could no longer pay off your credit card balance?
- What emotions would be triggered if your bank account was garnished?
- Have you looked into credit counseling or debt management counseling? (See **Urban Legend 24**). for a discussion on credit counseling services.
- Have you had collections actions taken against you for "zombie debt" that you previously paid off or that is not yours?

Urban Legend Number 13: A CREDIT CARD ISSUER CAN AUTOMATICALLY GARNISH MY BANK ACCOUNT IF I STOP PAYING ON MY CREDIT CARD.

URBAN LEGEND – 14

I can max out my credit
cards if I am going to
declare bankruptcy.

124

Urban Legend Number 14: I have a large credit card balance that I am having trouble paying. I have decided to declare bankruptcy. Since I have not exceeded my credit limit I am going to use my remaining credit balance to go on vacation and take out a cash advance. Since I am going to declare bankruptcy anyways, I can do whatever I want with my credit cards.

The Reality: _False._

Millions of people declare bankruptcy each year. In 2011, 1.36 million non-business bankruptcy filings were reported in the United States federal courts.[12] According to data released by the US Courts website in November 2012, non-business bankruptcies decreased by 14 percent in fiscal year 2012 (for a total of 1.26 million).[13] Bankruptcies are filed to stop collection actions and collection calls, discharge debt, and reorganize finances.

For individuals, there are two types of bankruptcies that can be filed in a federal bankruptcy court in the United States: Chapter 7 and Chapter 13.

Chapter 7 of Title 11 of the United States Code (U.S.C.)[14] defines a _liquidation_ process under the Bankruptcy Laws of the United States.

Chapter 13 of Title 11 of the U.S.C.[15] defines a _debt reorganization_ process and repayment plan under the Bankruptcy Laws of United States.

When a consumer files a bankruptcy case in the United States, a _Trustee_ is appointed, either by the United States Department of Justice, or by creditors involved in the bankruptcy case. The Trustee helps ensure that both the creditors' and the debtor's interests are maintained in accordance with the bankruptcy laws. The Trustee also functions as a negotiator between the debtor and the creditors.

Individuals who file bankruptcy under Chapter 7 are allowed to keep certain assets (i.e., exempt assets) while other assets (non-exempt) are sold to pay off creditors. There are instances when an individual who files bankruptcy under Chapter 7 is forced to involuntarily convert the filing into a Chapter 13 based on the individual's conduct. Such conduct includes running up credit card debt immediately before filing a bankruptcy.

Many bankruptcy Trustees are arguing that some credit card debt is <u>not</u> dischargeable in bankruptcy courts under either of two legal theories:

1. The credit card application *submitted* to get the card was submitted with an intent to commit fraudulent acts; or
2. The credit card *was used* with an intent to defraud the credit card company and without an intent to repay the debt incurred from the purchases made before filing bankruptcy.

Generally, the longer the length of time between any particular credit card use and the bankruptcy filing, the less likely the usage will trigger a challenge to dischargeability by a bankruptcy Trustee.

Urban Legend Number 14: I CAN MAX OUT MY CREDIT CARDS IF I AM GOING TO DECLARE BANKRUPTCY.

A complaint filed by a bankruptcy Trustee for non-dischargeability based on fraudulent application and use of a credit card (Theory No. 1) may seek non-dischargeability for certain charges, but not necessarily the entire balance. A consumer filing a Chapter 7 bankruptcy may have it involuntarily converted to a Chapter 13 to repay the charges that were not discharged.

However, a complaint by a bankruptcy Trustee based on an intent to defraud (Theory No. 2) may seek non-dischargeability of the entire credit card debt across all credit cards and force the consumer to repay it all. A consumer filing a Chapter 7 bankruptcy may have it involuntarily converted to a Chapter 13 to repay such alleged credit card fraud.

The bankruptcy code states that consumer debts owed to a single creditor and aggregating more than $550 for luxury goods or services incurred by an individual debtor on or within 90 days before the bankruptcy is filed are presumed to be non-dischargeable under Chapter 7[16].

Be careful about paying any creditor before filing a bankruptcy, as the bankruptcy code also states that a total of $600 or more in money or property which is paid to a creditor, a relative, or a friend within 90 days prior to bankruptcy filing is a called a *preference*. The bankruptcy Trustee may recover preferences and divide the money between all creditors[17].

A bankruptcy Trustee routinely considers the following factors and many others to determine if credit card purchases are dischargeable or not:

- Was the credit card newly issued?
- Were any large cash advances taken out with the credit card?
- Was the credit card used for recent travel or vacations?
- Was the credit card limit recently exceeded?
- Was the borrowing pattern on the credit card suddenly different?
- Was a cash advance from one credit card used to pay off another credit card?
- Was the credit card holder unemployed and used the credit card without a reasonable belief that the credit card debt could be repaid?

So, if you were tempted to make purchases with your credit card before a bankruptcy filing, don't! It is not worth the risk of non-dischargeability of your debt and your ability to make a fresh start.

Individuals who file bankruptcy under Chapter 13 are allowed to keep most assets. However, the debtor is required to propose a plan to pay his/her creditors off over a three to five year period. The plan must be approved by the bankruptcy court and is administered by an appointed Trustee.

The type and amount of *exempt assets* varies in each state. You will need to consult with a bankruptcy attorney in your own state to determine the specifics of exempt assets available to you.

In general, *exempt assets* include such items as a motor vehicle up to a certain value; equity in a home up to a certain value; household furnishings, appliances and clothing reasonably necessary for a debtor to live; and tools of the debtor's trade reasonably necessary for a debtor to work up to a certain value.

Secured creditors are paid first. If there is any money left over, then *unsecured creditors* are paid. A *secured creditor* is a creditor who claims a security interest in real property or personal property. Real property is land, and personal property is anything else you own. An *unsecured creditor* holds debt without collateral to secure the loan.

A secured creditor has a security interest in property and *protects* that interest by filing legal documents. For example, a secured creditor for an automobile loan files a lien on a title for the vehicle. A secured creditor for a mortgage files a lien on the title for real-estate. The lien is recorded in the local county clerk's office.

The Trustee appointed for Chapter 7 bankruptcy cases collects the debtor's non-exempt assets, sells the assets, pays sale expenses, and proportionally distributes the sale proceeds — first to secured creditors, and then to unsecured creditors if any proceeds remain.

The Trustee appointed for Chapter 13 bankruptcy cases receives the debtor's monthly payments and distributes the payments proportionally to the debtor's creditors based on the Chapter 13 repayment plan approved by the bankruptcy court.

Polly's Pearls of Wisdom: Filing bankruptcy will have a large impact on your credit score. When a Chapter 7 or Chapter 13 bankruptcy is filed, a person with a credit score of 680 would lose 130-150 points, while a person with a credit score of 780 would lose 220-240 points.

A Chapter 7 bankruptcy filing stays on a person's credit report for ten years. A Chapter 13 bankruptcy filing stays on a person's credit report for seven years.

Do not rely on the use of bankruptcy filing for credit card debt management. The amount of time until you can file for another bankruptcy varies from two to eight years depending on the type of bankruptcy filed.

- If your first bankruptcy filing was a Chapter 7, you must wait eight years from the filing date of your first Chapter 7 bankruptcy before you can file another Chapter 7 bankruptcy[18].
- If your first bankruptcy filing was a Chapter 7 and your second bankruptcy filing is a Chapter 13, you have to wait four years.
- If your first bankruptcy filing was a Chapter 13, you have to wait two years before filing a second Chapter 13.

Urban Legend Number 14: I CAN MAX OUT MY CREDIT CARDS IF I AM GOING TO DECLARE BANKRUPTCY.

- If your first bankruptcy filing was a Chapter 13, and you desire to file a Chapter 7, you have to wait six years.

Many consumers have tried to make new and expensive purchases before declaring bankruptcy. These consumers make purchases for products or services they feel are transitory or cannot be undone. For example, they make purchases such as taking the family on a foreign vacation, going a cruise in a first class cabin, paying for cosmetic surgery procedures, or having cosmetic dental procedures.

These consumers feel that if they are going to declare bankruptcy and have their credit score drop hundreds of points, they can make purchases on their credit cards to "max" out the cards and just discharge the debt.

But BEWARE! Most bankruptcy courts are placing credit card debt and credit card charges under a very high level of scrutiny. The Trustee overseeing the bankruptcy case can file to have purchases declared non-dischargeable, and the consumer will be held liable for these purchases.

A consumer in such a situation that intended to file a Chapter 7 bankruptcy may be forced to file a Chapter 13 bankruptcy and pay back the credit card companies for all their purchases.

If you are considering bankruptcy, consult with a bankruptcy attorney in your area before making any decisions. Be sure to also consult with your accountant and your financial advisor.

In addition, you may want to seek credit counseling before or after filing bankruptcy (see **Urban Legend 24**).

As was discussed for **Urban Legend 8**, the NFCC is a non-profit agency with credit counseling experts who are specifically trained to help you with your debt management. For more information on NFCC credit counseling, visit (www.nfcc.org) or call (800)388-2227 (see **Urban Legend 24**).

There is a commercial that is aired on many television stations for a bankruptcy attorney who has a multi-state practice. In this advertisement, the attorney states, "filing bankruptcy is like going to the dentist." He goes on to say, "everybody fears it and it may hurt, but after you go, you feel much better."

Deciding to file for bankruptcy, filing, and dealing with the aftermath is very likely to bring up many different negative emotions and negative feelings.

A number of different positive emotions may also surface when you stop receiving collections notices, collections telephone calls, and overdue bills; and when the burden of debt is removed or made bearable.

Ask yourself the following questions.

Plastic Reactions:

- How did you feel when you decided to declare bankruptcy?
- How did you feel after you went to bankruptcy court?
- How did you feel about the decrease in your credit score?
- Do you regret any impulsive purchases you made before declaring bankruptcy that were ruled non-dischargeable?
- Do you feel better with the stress of unpaid debt being removed or being reorganized so you can afford to pay for your debt?
- What new habits can you learn to prevent yourself from being in this situation in the future? Write down a list of ideas and implement them as soon as possible.

URBAN LEGEND – 15

A cash advance with my credit card is the same as taking out cash from an ATM.

Urban Legend Number 15: I frequently use my credit card to take out a cash advance. The cash advance is no different than taking money out of my bank account with an ATM card.

The Reality: *False.*

Cash advances are actually loans provided to you by your credit card issuer. Cash advance loans include fees and very high compound interest rates. For example, if your APR for purchases for your credit card was 13.24 percent, the APR for cash advances may be 20.24 percent.

The fees for cash advances typically range from 2 to 4 percent of the cash advance amount, with an average cash advance fee of about 3 percent. Many credit card issuers charge a minimum cash advance fee of $10 or more.

So, if you used your credit card to withdraw $100, your fee would be $10, since 3 percent of $100 is $3 and this is less than the $10 minimum fee. Also, your interest rate for the cash advance would be 20.24 percent. The interest rate for cash advances is also a compound interest rate.

Compare this to the charges you would incur by withdrawing money from your bank account with your debit card or ATM card. Your only charge would be the ATM fee of $1-$3, if any fee was charged at all.

The CARD Act of 2009 made it more difficult for credit card issuers to profit from cash advances on credit cards by limiting the number of fees that can be charged to an account per month, and by requiring banks to apply any monies received over the minimum payment to the portion of the balance with the highest interest rate.

Polly's Pearls of Wisdom: Cash advances are treated very differently than purchases made with credit cards. When a credit card holder makes purchases, the purchases are accumulated for a billing cycle, which is typically 31 days. If the credit card holder pays off his/her balance in full at the end of the billing cycle, no interest charges are charged to the credit card holder.

What many credit card holders don't realize is that if they take out a cash advance with their credit card, interest is charged from the moment the cash is received. There is no grace period for interest charges charged on cash advances.

If your credit score is low, the interest rate charged for cash advances could reach the maximum allowed by law.

If you take out a cash advance and cannot pay off your credit card balance in full, you should make sure to pay more than the minimum payment. The CARD Act of 2009 requires credit card issuers to apply any monies received above the minimum payment amount to the portion of the balance being charged the highest interest rate. This will help you to decrease the amount of interest you are paying per month more quickly than if you just make the minimum payment.

Urban Legend 15: A CASH ADVANCE FROM MY CREDIT CARD IS THE SAME AS TAKING OUT CASH FROM AN ATM.

Many credit card issuers routinely send credit card holders courtesy checks to make it easy and tempting for a credit card holder to take out a cash advance. Many credit card issuers send these courtesy checks out on a monthly basis.

My advice to you is that when you receive such courtesy checks, immediately walk directly to your shredder and drop them in. You can also call your credit card issuer and request that they stop sending you these courtesy checks. This also removes a potential source of fraud, because the courtesy checks can potentially be stolen from your mailbox.

If you are tempted to withdraw a cash advance using your credit card, carefully consider the situation. A cash advance using your credit card should always be treated as an *emergency* or *last resort* type of action. It should never be done for day-to-day or impulse purchases.

Plastic Reactions:

- Did a negative or positive emotion trigger the desire for a cash advance? Identify this emotion and think about how you might have avoided the cash advance and its associated costs if you were able to control this emotional trigger.

- Was it an emergency situation that created your need for a cash advance? Do you have a sound financial plan for emergency situations that may arise in your life?
- If you are in an emergency situation, can you get the money from another source such as a friend, family member, or even your own bank account?
- Do you actually need the cash to make a purchase? If so, you should make the purchase without taking out the cash advance, if possible. If you have reached your available credit limit on purchases, can you delay the purchase until you have the available credit?
- Can you pay the cash advance off at the end of the month?
- Did you realize how much the cash advance would cost you in fees and interest?
- Will you think differently about using cash advances on your credit card in the future after reading this chapter?

Urban Legend 15: A CASH ADVANCE FROM MY CREDIT CARD IS THE SAME AS TAKING OUT CASH FROM AN ATM.

URBAN LEGEND – 16

My credit limits will automatically increase each time I get a new job at a higher salary.

Urban Legend Number 16: I just received a promotion at work and am receiving a larger salary. My credit limits will automatically be increased on my credit cards.

The Reality: *False.*

Credit card issuers will not automatically raise your credit limit based on you receiving a larger salary. Salary information is not routinely reported to the credit reporting bureaus and thus is not included on your credit reports. Since salary information is not included on your credit report, it does not affect your credit score.

However, for other types of applications for credit (such those for mortgages, vehicle loans, etc.), salary information is very relevant and is routinely requested, reported, and considered. Thus, in some circumstances, your employment history may be reported to the three credit reporting bureaus and appear on your credit reports. However, most employment histories on credit reports are almost never updated and thus most are very out-of-date.

For example, you may have started to work at a company in the mail room as an hourly employee while you were finishing your college degree. When you graduated, you applied for and were hired for a group leader position as a salaried employee. The employment history section on your credit report is likely to note only your start date at your company, and not your job titles or promotions.

If your employment history is reported on your credit reports, it may be used by credit card issuers to confirm an income level and such information could be used to set a credit limit when a credit card application for a credit card is approved.

Most credit card applications ask for an annual salary or monthly salary. Credit card issuers use tables that include a range of credit scores and annual gross incomes that are used to approve or deny a credit card application. Many credit card issuers use two main factors in the credit card application approval process and credit limit determination: current credit score and current gross annual income.

As was discussed for **Urban Legend Number 7**, if you need a higher credit limit you should call your credit card issuer and ask for one. Your new job at a higher salary may make your eligible for a higher credit limit.

Polly's Pearls of Wisdom: As you climb the corporate ladder, get a better job, and improve your lifestyle, you need to use these improvements to reduce your debt.

"Old-school" financial theory recommended that when you receive a raise, you should pay off your credit cards with the highest interest rates first, until your debt is gone. By doing this, you <u>really</u> give yourself a double raise. This is still excellent advice today.

You didn't have the extra money before receiving the raise, and if you use the money to increase your credit card payments, you will reduce your debt quickly. As one credit card is paid off, use the money that is no longer needed to pay that card and double the payment on your card with the next highest interest rate. When that card is paid off, then triple the payment being made on your next highest card, and so on, until your debt is gone. Your credit score will also increase over time.

You should also consider whether or not you actually need a higher credit limit. Remember, as was discussed in **Urban Legend Number 10**, a higher credit limit on a credit card will affect the *credit utilization* component that comprises 30 percent of your credit score. As was discussed for **Urban Legends 7 and 10**, the impact of credit utilization on your credit score varies depending on your credit history.

Remember, to keep your credit scores high, keep your *credit utilization* scores low. With a higher credit limit, it is tempting to spend more. So don't ask for a higher credit limit unless you actually need it.

Plastic Reactions:

- Did your promotion trigger any positive emotions? If so, which ones? Did it trigger any negative emotions?

- Now that you are making more money, are you going out to immediately purchase something new as a reward or a celebration? Will it be something expensive?
- Will your promotion affect the way you view your credit cards and debt management? If so, how?
- How can you use this new income to give yourself financial freedom? Can you double or triple your credit card payments and become debt free faster?
- Have you consulted with your financial planner to update your plan for your finances now that your income has increased? Have you examined your budget? This sort of planning can put you on the path towards financial freedom and a comfortable retirement.

Urban Legend 16: MY CREDIT LIMITS WILL AUTOMATICALLY INCREASE EACH TIME I GET A NEW JOB AT A HIGHER SALARY.

URBAN LEGEND – 17

I am not responsible for the credit card debt of my children as a co-signer on their credit cards.

Urban Legend Number 17: My eighteen-year-old daughter wanted a credit card, but could not obtain one without a co-signer. My daughter used her credit card to buy $5,000 worth of new clothing and accessories and has stopped making payments on her credit card. I am not responsible for her credit card debt and my credit scores will not go down.

The Reality: *False.*

Young adults between the ages of 18 and 20 cannot typically receive a credit card unless an adult over age 21 co-signs the application or the young adult can prove the ability to pay his/her own debts.

A co-signing parent or other adult is legally responsible for all credit card debt incurred by a minor child. Be aware that laws governing the legal age of adulthood vary by state. Late payments or non-payments made on the co-signed card will appear on both the minor child's and the parent's credit reports. Both the minor child's and the parent's credit scores are also directly affected by the activity on the co-signed credit card.

New Federal Reserve Laws enacted in 2010 and the Credit Card Accountability, Responsibility, and Disclosure (CARD) Act of 2009 include provisions to help young consumers better control and incur less credit card debt. Based on the new laws, if a credit card applicant under the age of 21 cannot prove the ability to repay, they must have a co-signer.

Polly's Pearls of Wisdom: Think carefully about your reasoning for co-signing a credit card. Is it to establish credit for someone going to college? Is it to teach them to manage money? Be aware that when you co-sign a credit card for a young adult, you will be liable if they are unable or unwilling to pay for the debt accumulated on this credit card. Parents should also be willing to accept the consequences of a lower credit score, which would result if the co-signed card was misused.

All parents who co-sign a credit card application for a minor child should closely monitor the credit card debt incurred on this credit card. If the cardholder is making too many purchases and is accumulating too much credit card debt, the parent should immediately intervene to stop and correct the situation before it reaches a critical level.

Parents can also use such situations to teach their children about financial responsibility. Young adults can be prevented from developing unrealistic expectations such as: there are no consequences to making poor financial decisions, and their parents will always be there to bail them out.

If you are a parent and you are going to co-sign for a credit card for a minor child, many credit card issuers offer low credit limit (e.g., $250) cards specifically for minor children. If your child has not applied for such a credit card, call the credit card issuer and request the credit card have a small credit limit (e.g., $200 - $500). Choose a value you would be comfortable paying if the

Urban Legend Number 17: I AM NOT RESPONSIBLE FOR THE CREDIT CARD DEBT OF MY CHILDREN AS A CO-SIGNER ON THEIR CREDIT CARDS.

card was charged to its limit by your child. Also, request that the credit limit not be changed without your permission as the adult co-signer, and that any purchases attempted over the credit limit be automatically denied.

Such actions limit the risk associated with co-signing for a credit card for your minor child, yet allow him/her to use the credit card and learn financial responsibility.

Plastic Reactions:

- How would you feel if your minor child asked you to co-sign a credit card application for a credit card with a $500 credit limit? How about a card with a $5,000 credit limit?
- What concerns or questions would arise for you if your child requested your help getting a credit card while he/she was away at college? What if he/she still lived at home?
- What emotions would be triggered if your child exceeded a credit limit on a credit card for which you co-signed the application?
- How would you react if your credit score went down based on your minor child's spending habits with the credit card you co-signed?

- Would your own emotional reactions be influenced depending on your child's emotional reactions? For example, if your child were genuinely remorseful about spending beyond his or her credit limit, would that impact your own emotional reactions? What if your child were unaffected by exceeding the credit limit?
- If your child's actions with a co-signed credit card caused your own credit score to go down, how would you feel about helping your child with financial issues that may arise in the future?

Urban Legend Number 17: I AM NOT RESPONSIBLE FOR THE CREDIT CARD DEBT OF MY CHILDREN AS A CO-SIGNER ON THEIR CREDIT CARDS.

URBAN LEGEND – 18

I am not responsible for the credit card debt of a deceased spouse.

Urban Legend Number 18: My spouse passed away, leaving a large amount of credit card debt on our one credit card. My spouse accumulated all of the credit card debt. However, the credit card was issued in both of our names, and I was a co-signer on the credit card application. Since I did not incur any of the credit card debt, I am not responsible for paying it off because my spouse is deceased.

The Reality: _False._

Since you signed the credit card application as a co-signer and a joint account holder, you will be held liable for the debt, along with the estate of your spouse.

However, if you had signed the credit card application as an authorized user instead of a co-signer, even if you had charging privileges on the card you would not be responsible for the credit card debt.

The estate of a deceased person consists of all real and personal property owned by the person at the time of death. If the estate goes into court and through probate as the result of the deceased having left or not left a _Last Will and Testament_ (i.e., a Will), a probate administrator or executor will look at the assets and debts of the deceased, and, as guided by state law, determine in what order bills (including credit card bills) should be paid. Remaining assets are then distributed to heirs based on the Will or the state's intestate-related legal statutes.

A credit card issuer can't legally force someone else to pay credit card debt for a deceased person if they have not co-signed on the credit card account. Children, friends, or relatives of a deceased person can not inherit credit card debt.

Polly's Pearls of Wisdom: It is a good idea to make a list of all your credit cards, including the issuers' contact information and your credit card account numbers.

Such a list is valuable in the event of a death or in the event a wallet or purse has been stolen. Put a copy of the list in your safety deposit box and keep a copy in safe place at home for easy reference.

If your spouse has passed away, the CARD Act of 2009 now requires the credit card issuers to provide a final credit card balance in a timely manner when requested by an executor of an estate after the death of a cardholder. The CARD Act also requires credit card issuers to immediately stop charging all late fees, non-payment fees, and all other fees during the time period an executor is trying to settle a credit card account after the death of a cardholder.

Unfortunately the FTC enacted new rules[19] in 2011 giving debt collectors more freedom to contact the spouses, children, friends, and relatives of the deceased. Many debt collectors routinely set up obituary-watching services, and map names of the deceased to those with delinquent accounts in their own databases. It is routine procedure for many debt collectors to immediately call the widow or family of the deceased, and, at a time when the widow or family is grieving and not thinking clearly, demand payment of the outstanding debt.

The debt collection rules vary greatly from state-to-state. So check the rules for your state to determine what debt collectors can and cannot do when trying to collect the debt of a deceased loved one.

In reality, most credit card debt is unsecured debt and credit card issuers are considered *unsecured creditors* (See **Urban Legend 14**). So, if a dispute arose between an estate of a deceased person and a credit card issuer, it is very unlikely a credit card issuer would be able to collect the credit card debt from the estate of the deceased.

As part of your estate planning, you should consider options other than a Will. A Will can go into probate and be subject to the FTC rules and other probate rules. When a Will is admitted to probate, it becomes a public document as part of the public court record for anyone to see and read. Many probate courts put all Wills online so they are available via the Internet to everyone all the time.

When you do your estate planning, consider establishing trusts and other legal entities (other than Wills) that can privately control assets after a person dies. As there are many tax advantages to creating trusts instead of using Wills, be sure to discuss the matter with your accountant or financial planner as well as with your estate planning attorney.

A death or other major loss, such as the loss of a home or job, is likely to trigger many different emotions, including many negative emotions. In spite of the situation, try to stay as aware as possible of who is contacting you and what they are asking. Don't be afraid to ask for help during the grieving process.

Whether you are grieving the loss of a loved one, the loss of your home, or the loss of your financial stability, it's important to be aware that the feelings that accompany your grief are legitimate.

The *Kübler-Ross Model* developed by Elisabeth Kübler-Ross, also known as *The Five Stages of Grief*,[20] suggests that everyone experiences the following five emotional and mental stages when grieving a loss or facing their own impending death. These stages include:

- Denial – "This cannot be happening."
- Anger – "This isn't fair! I need to blame someone!"
- Bargaining – "I'll do anything you ask if you can keep this person with me for longer."
- Depression – "There's no reason to go on now."
- Acceptance – "I can deal with this, even if it's not easy."

Take some time to reflect on your current emotional state. Consider your reactions to situations like attempts made to collect the debt of your loved one. See if you can identify any changes in your usual reactions to this type of situation. You may find clues to help you identify if your behavior is being affected by these stages of grief.

Plastic Reactions:

- Are you grieving the loss of a loved one, the loss of a job, the loss of your home, or some other impending loss?
- Can you identify any of these grief stages that you have already experienced or are currently experiencing?

There are many organizations that assist with the grieving process, both for loss of a family member and for other major life transitions. Whether you are grieving from a death or grieving from financial loss, there are resources available to help you. Here are just a few of the organizations you could contact:

- **The Association for Death Education and Counseling** - This is a large interdisciplinary organization that focuses on dying and bereavement. Members include medical and mental health professionals, clergy members, educators, and volunteers. Their website can help you find a specialist ideal for your needs. Their website: (www.adec.org).

- **AARP Grief and Loss Programs** – AARP offers a variety of resources for dealing with many kinds of grief, including online forums, local partnerships, brochures and other publications. Their website: (www.aarp.org/relationships/grief-loss).
- **National Hospice and Palliative Care Organization** – This nonprofit group is dedicated to quality, compassionate, end-of-life care and has an informative website with lots of helpful information. Their website: (www.nhpco.org).
- **Center for Loss and Life Transition** – This group provides support for mourners, caregivers, and supporters. They offer local training and other resources to assist with the grieving process on all fronts. Their website: (www.centerforloss.com).

Urban Legend Number 18: I AM NOT RESPONSIBLE FOR THE CREDIT CARD DEBT OF A DECEASED SPOUSE.

URBAN LEGEND – 19

Credit card issuers can automatically close credit card accounts upon the death of a spouse.

Urban Legend Number 19: I have been a homemaker for the last forty years. All of our credit cards were joint credit cards in both of our names and we were both co-signers even though I did not work outside the home. We have paid all our credit cards each month and have no credit card debt. My husband recently passed away. The credit card issuer can cancel our credit cards and close our accounts because I am an older woman and I don't have a job.

The Reality: _False._
When your spouse dies, you should notify your credit card issuers as soon as possible. Each credit card issuer will likely ask you to mail or fax a copy of the death certificate for your deceased spouse. When you send the death certificate, be sure to include a letter of explanation including the deceased's account number to avoid confusion. Be sure to include you own contact information. Send it via registered or certified mail so you can be sure it was actually delivered and received by the credit reporting bureaus.

You should also notify each of the three credit reporting agencies after a death. Each credit reporting agency puts a death notice on the deceased's credit file to avoid identity theft or fraud issues. To place a death notice on a credit file, mail a copy of the death certificate to each of three credit reporting agencies via certified or registered mail to ensure delivery.

Upon notification, a credit card issuer may ask you to update your credit application or reapply if the initial acceptance of the application was based on all or part of your spouse's income, and if the credit card issuer has reason to suspect your income is inadequate to support the current credit limits on the credit cards.

However, do not worry, because there are laws against credit discrimination in such circumstances. The FTC enforces the Equal Credit Opportunity Act[21] (ECOA) to prevent credit discrimination on the basis of sex, marital status, and age (and race, color, religion, national origin, or because of receipt of public assistance).

A woman may not be denied credit just because she is a woman, is widowed (or married, single, divorced, or separated), or is elderly. As long as she shows that she is creditworthy and falls into the guidelines of the credit application she originally signed, she can't be discriminated against and her credit cannot be canceled.

If a credit card issuer does require you to reapply for your credit cards, you can continue to use your credit cards up to your credit limit with no restrictions until you receive a response to the reapplication. The credit card issuer must provide a response to your reapplication, and, if they deny your application, they must provide a written reason for the denial.

Notifying the credit card issuers and the three reporting agencies will also help prevent identity theft after the death of a spouse.

Urban Legend Number 19: CREDIT CARD ISSUERS CAN AUTOMATICALLY CLOSE CREDIT CARD ACCOUNTS UPON THE DEATH OF A SPOUSE.

Unfortunately, many criminals also read obituaries and target people they believe may be vulnerable to social engineering from which they can likely obtain personal information such as credit card numbers, social security numbers, etc.

Such personal information is then used to make additional purchases on the deceased's credit cards, and can significantly increase credit card debt.

Polly's Pearls of Wisdom: Please understand that we are addressing this from the standpoint of a female homemaker posing the question. However, the discussion is also relevant for a male homemaker. Every woman, whether married, single, divorced, or separated, should have at least one credit card solely in her own name. If she is married, and, if anything happens to her spouse and the family credit is in the husband's name alone, she may not easily be able to establish credit for herself.

This is especially true in the case of a homemaker, who may not have worked for decades, or who is suddenly widowed (or divorced) with no job or new source of income.

If your spouse passes away and you did not work, or you do work and your income was significantly less than your spouse's, you will likely receive a new credit card with a lower credit limit.

If your credit cards were only in the name of your deceased spouse, the accounts were not joint accounts, and you were an authorized user but not a co-signer, you should get a copy of your credit reports from the three credit reporting bureaus. If you never established any credit, your credit reports may have no credit information listed or may say "no records found." (**See Urban Legend 18**).

How do you establish credit in such a situation? Find a credit card issuer that offers a *secured credit card*. Most credit cards, and all of the credit cards discussed up to this point, are *unsecured credit cards*. An unsecured credit card does not require any collateral (e.g., money or property) be secured before the card is issued and used.

A *secured credit card* is a credit card that requires collection of some type of collateral before use. The most common type of collateral is money in a designated account (i.e., a savings or money market account). When money is deposited in the designated account, the amount of money on deposit becomes your credit limit on the associated secured credit card account.

Unlike an unsecured credit card, a credit limit on a secured credit card may be variable. You can request an increase in your credit limit by depositing more money as collateral. Sometimes the issuing bank will reward a good payment history by increasing your credit line to an amount above what you have deposited as collateral.

Urban Legend Number 19: CREDIT CARD ISSUERS CAN AUTOMATICALLY CLOSE CREDIT CARD ACCOUNTS UPON THE DEATH OF A SPOUSE.

The secured credit card is used just like an unsecured credit card. Purchases are made, credit card bills are sent, payments are made, and on-time or late payments are usually reported to the credit bureaus.

Your available credit limit can also vary if you do not pay your charges in full each month.[22] For example, if you deposited $250 in the bank account for your secured credit card, your credit limit would be $250. If you spent the $200 of the $250 and made a payment of only $50, your available credit limit would be $100 and not $250 ($250 - $200 = $50 + $50 = $100). You would be charged interest on the outstanding balance of $150, and your credit limit would not return to $250 until the balance was paid in full.

This is similar to making a minimum payment on an unsecured credit card and carrying a balance forward to the next billing cycle, which causes you to pay interest and lowers your available credit limit.

Almost all secured cards report your credit payment history to the three credit reporting bureaus each month.

To build or re-build your credit, it is advisable to try and obtain several secured credit cards, make small purchases on each, and pay them off on time and in full each month.

A list of secured credit card issuers can be found online at Bank Rate (www.bankrate.com). This site compares features and fees associated with the secured credit cards being offered. Many major banks and credit unions offer secured credit cards.

Bank Rate also has an informative article on their website called "10 questions before getting secured credit cards" (www.bankrate.com/finance/cards/10-questions-before-getting-a-secured-credit-card). This article contains important basic information about secured credit cards and what to keep in mind when you compare credit card offers.

Responsible use of a secured credit card will allow you to build a positive credit history, and will increase your creditworthiness and your credit score.

If you have applied for an unsecured credit card and your application has been denied, you can use a secured credit card to build your credit so you will eventually become eligible to apply for and obtain an unsecured credit card again.

Secured credit cards are often used by consumers who have filed bankruptcy (See **Urban Legend 14**) to try to re-establish their credit history and improve their credit scores.

Urban Legend Number 19: CREDIT CARD ISSUERS CAN AUTOMATICALLY CLOSE CREDIT CARD ACCOUNTS UPON THE DEATH OF A SPOUSE.

Plastic Reactions:

- If you shared a credit history with someone who is no longer with you, what emotions did you feel when you realized you did not establish any credit history for yourself?
- What emotions would you experience if your credit card issuer asked you to reapply for your own credit card, or issued you a new credit card with a much lower credit limit?
- How would you feel if you applied for a credit card solely in your own name in the first year of marriage to establish and protect your own credit history? How would you feel if your spouse did the same?
- What emotions would you feel if you had to apply for a secured credit card in order to establish or grow your credit? How would you feel if you were able to transfer to an unsecured card later?

URBAN LEGEND – 20

Never checking my credit
score and credit reports
has no consequences.

Urban Legend Number 20: I have several credit cards. I always pay off my balance at the end of the month. I have never made a late payment or missed a payment and I have a good job. I have never obtained a copy of my credit reports or my credit scores. I wanted to move into a new apartment and my lease application was denied. The denial of my apartment lease application has absolutely nothing to do with my credit score or what is on my credit reports.

The Reality: *False.*

Although there may be many other reasons that your lease application was denied, the denial may be the direct result of errors on your credit reports that have affected your credit score.

As was discussed in the **What is a Credit Report?** section, a large number of credit reports include errors. Such errors directly affect your credit score. Since you did not obtain a current copy of your credit reports, you were not aware of any errors.

Errors on your credit report can occur if a creditor makes an error and reports the error to the credit reporting bureau. Errors can also occur when mistakes are made by the credit reporting bureaus during their data entry process. You should request your free credit reports from the three major credit reporting bureaus once per year and check them for errors, and dispute any errors you may find as discussed in the **What is a Credit Report?** section.

Polly's Pearls of Wisdom: How often do errors occur? More often than you might think. While credit reporting companies claim that most of their reports do not have errors, a 2004 study by The Federation of State Public Interest Research Groups (PIRG) found that nearly 79% of all credit reports contained at least one type of error.[23]

More recently, the *Columbus Dispatch* conducted a year-long investigation (published in 2012) into credit report errors and examined nearly 30,000 customer complaints with the FTC, finding an error rate of about 30%[24]. The complaints were over errors ranging from incorrect personal information to completely inaccurate debt information. Some credit reports even had the consumers listed as deceased when they were very much alive!

Both creditors and the credit reporting bureaus are responsible for accepting and reporting a huge amount of data. As much as they try to be accurate, mistakes happen. It is up to you to catch and correct those mistakes on your own credit report, and even then, you must be persistent. In more than half of the complaints investigated by the *Columbus Dispatch*, consumers reported that the major credit reporting companies could not be convinced to correct the errors on their credit reports.

Urban Legend Number 20: NEVER CHECKING MY CREDIT SCORE
AND CREDIT REPORTS HAS NO CONSEQUENCES.

Fortunately, recent changes have given consumers more options for dealing with credit report errors. *The Washington Post* reports that the Consumer Financial Protection Bureau (CFPB) now accepts complaints about credit reporting companies, and is investigating errors in reports as well as improper use of reports and the struggles that some people have even getting their reports.[25]

If you request your credit report and see errors on it, first try to get the errors resolved with the credit reporting company by going through their complaint process (see **What is a Credit Report?** section). If that fails, contact the CFPB either by going online to (www.consumerfinance.gov/complaint), or by calling toll-free (855)411-2372. You can also fax complaints to (855)237-2392, or mail them to Consumer Financial Protection Bureau, P.O. Box 4503, Iowa City, Iowa, 52244.

Plastic Reactions:

- Are you afraid to look at your three credit bureau reports?
- Are you avoiding facing reality?
- What emotions did you feel when you found out that errors on your credit reports caused your application for an apartment lease to be denied?
- Will the denial change your behavior with respect to your credit score and credit reports?

- Will this denial action impact how you handle your credit reports in the future?
- Do you now know what to do if you find an error in your credit report?
- Are you willing to assign your credit health to a computer program instead of taking responsibility yourself?

Urban Legend Number 20: NEVER CHECKING MY CREDIT SCORE AND CREDIT REPORTS HAS NO CONSEQUENCES.

URBAN LEGEND – 21

I am not liable for any fraudulent charges if my credit card is stolen.

Urban Legend Number 21: My wallet was stolen with my credit cards inside. There is no hurry to report my credit cards as stolen, and I am not liable for any fraudulent charges made by the thief on my credit cards.

The Reality: *False.*

Always report any theft of your credit cards to your credit card issuers as soon as possible. The Fair Credit Billing Act (FCBA) is a federal law in the United States that defines rules for stolen credit cards.[26]

Under the FCBA, if you report the theft of your credit cards before any unauthorized charges are made, you have zero dollars of financial responsibility.

If a thief uses your stolen cards before they are reported stolen to the credit card issuers, your maximum financial liability is $50. However, most credit card issuers have a zero liability policy and will not try to collect the $50 from you.

The rules for debit cards and ATM cards are VERY different. So if your wallet included any debit cards or ATM cards, you must act immediately. The Electronic Fund Transfer Act (EFTA) is a federal law in the United States that defines rules for stolen debit cards and ATM cards.[27]

Your financial liability for unauthorized use of a debit card or ATM card is directly dependent on how quickly you report the loss.[28]

If you report the loss within two (2) business days after your card is stolen or missing, you will not be responsible for more than $50 for unauthorized use.

However, if you don't report the loss within two business days after theft or loss, you could be responsible for up to $500 because of an unauthorized transfer.

If your debit or ATM card is stolen or lost, and you fail to report an unauthorized transfer within 60 days after any statement including a listing of the unauthorized use is mailed to you, you could be responsible for an *unlimited* financial loss. The unlimited loss includes all the money in your account, plus any overdrafts over your credit limit on the account, and any overdraft fees associated with such overdrafts.

The rules are slightly different if you maintain possession of your card and only your credit card number is stolen. Credit card numbers and corresponding security codes are often stolen in restaurants, bars, and clubs when you hand your card to a server or bartender. When they walk away, they swipe your card to pay your bill, but also write down your credit card number and security code. An inexpensive card reader attached to a cell phone can also be used to swipe your card and record the information encoded in the magnetic strip into the memory of the cell phone. Such credit card numbers and security codes are often sold to organized crime rings, which use this information to make unauthorized purchases or re-sell it to others.

The FCBA states that if your credit card number was stolen and you are still in possession of the credit card and your number was used for unauthorized purchases, you have you have zero dollars of financial responsibility after your report the theft.

However, if your debit card or ATM card number is stolen and you maintain possession of the card, under the Electronic Fund Transfer Act (EFTA) you are liable for all unauthorized transfers if more than 60 days elapse after any statement including a listing of the unauthorized transfer is mailed to you and you did not report the loss of the number and the fraudulent activity.

Polly's Pearls of Wisdom: If your credit card is stolen, you absolutely should file a police report. Your loss may be very minor to local police investigators, but having a police report on file can protect you from future losses.

It is a very good idea to make a list of all your credit cards, debit cards, and ATM cards. On your list include the card number and expiration date, the name of the card issuer, and the card issuer's contact information.

If you do this and your cards are lost or stolen, you will have all the appropriate information you need to proceed. The FTC provides documents with checklists to follow if your credit card is stolen.[29]

Remember to keep the list in a safe place. If your house is burglarized, your list could provide the thief with a road map to all your cards!

If your credit card is stolen, also be careful what action you request your credit card issuer to take. When a credit card issuer receives a report about a stolen card, they will typically deactivate the stolen card and its associated credit card account. The credit card issuer will then issue a new or a replacement card with a new credit card number, and transfer your credit card balance to the new account for free. Such actions do not affect your credit score.

However, if you call your credit card issuer and request your card be *canceled* or your account closed, such actions typically will affect your credit score. If you have a balance on your credit card, closing the account will require you immediately pay off the outstanding balance in full.

Canceling a credit card or closing a credit card account can affect one or more of the following components of your credit score: credit utilization (30 percent), length of credit history (15 percent), types of credit used (10 percent), or new credit obtained (10 percent) (see **What is a Credit Score?** and **Urban Legend 7**). The exact number of points your credit score will drop varies and depends on your individual credit history and current credit score.

If you cancel a credit card or close an account and decide to apply for a new one, your application will generate a hard inquiry (See **Urban Legend 1**), which could further lower your credit scores.

If your credit card has been stolen, be diligent about monitoring your credit reports and your credit score. For a period of time, it is wise to put a freeze on your credit report, especially if you suspect identity theft. Be aware that you will need to monitor your

credit reports, and will need to have the freeze
removed at a later date.

You can contact the credit reporting bureaus
and ask them to put a *security freeze* on all your
current accounts listed on your credit report. The
credit reporting bureaus charge a fee (e.g., $15-$20)
for the start and end of the security freeze. The
security freeze stays in effect until you remove it.

When you freeze your credit report, creditors and
lenders can't check your credit reports or credit score
unless you've provided the credit reporting bureaus with
a password that is given to your current creditors and
lenders. If you try to apply for new credit, your
application will likely be denied because the new creditor
will not have the password and will not be able to access
your credit reports or credit score.

If your debit card or ATM card is stolen, you
must act immediately. Call your card issuer to report
the theft or loss, and follow up in writing, because the
rules governing debit cards and ATM cards can
subject you to unlimited financial liability as was
discussed previously.

The credit bureaus, credit card companies, and
other business organizations offer credit monitoring
services, identity theft monitoring, and identity theft
insurance. See **Urban Legend 4** for details regarding
these services.

Plastic Reactions:

- If you've recently suffered a credit card theft, how did the theft make you feel?
- If you haven't suffered a credit card theft, what emotions are triggered when you think about how such a theft could impact you?
- How would you feel knowing another person may be using your credit card to fraudulently make purchases?
- If your credit card has been stolen, how do you feel now when making purchases? Have your credit card habits changed because of the theft?
- Are you concerned about your potential liability for your debit and ATM cards?
- Do you feel empowered by knowing what the differences are for fraud liability between credit cards and debit or ATM cards?

Urban Legend Number 21: I AM NOT LIABLE FOR ANY FRAUDULENT CHARGES IF MY CREDIT CARD IS STOLEN.

URBAN LEGEND – 22

A credit repair agency can immediately raise my credit score.

Urban Legend Number 22: I made some bad decisions and incurred too much credit card debt. I missed many payments, and I eventually had to declare bankruptcy. My credit score plummeted hundreds of points. I found a credit repair agency that claims they can increase my credit score back to its former number in just a few months and remove all negative entries from my credit reports.

The Reality: _False_.

There are a large number of companies that target consumers who have poor credit histories with promises to clean up their credit reports. The truth is <u>no</u> company or individual can remove _negative, but accurate, information_ from your credit reports.

As was discussed throughout this book, accurate negative information remains on your credit report anywhere from two to ten years, depending on the type of negative entry. Most negative entries on your credit report remain there for seven years.

If you pay any credit repair agency any fees at all to repair your credit, the end result will be that you will have exactly the same credit score as you did before you started, you will have exactly the same accurate negative information on your credit reports, and you will have wasted any money you paid to the credit repair company.

Many credit repair companies will do nothing more than to assist you with the identification of inaccurate information and errors on your credit reports, and then charge you to complete the documentation to dispute the errors. This is something you can do yourself for free.

Remember, US Federal Law allows you to annually obtain a free copy of all three of your credit reports from the credit reporting bureaus. You can dispute any inaccurate or incomplete information in your credit report for free. The dispute procedure can even be done electronically directly from the webpages displaying the electronic copies of your credit reports. It can also be done on paper (see **What is a Credit Report?**).

Polly's Pearls of Wisdom: The Credit Repair Organizations Act[30] (CROA) helps protect you from credit repair scams. It prohibits a credit repair company from making false claims about its services, specifies that they can't make you pay until they complete the services they promise to you, and requires that they have your signature on a written contract before they can perform any services.

The CROA also provides for a three-day cancelation period for any written contract you may sign. However, since most credit repair organizations do not provide any services that you could not do yourself for free, you should think twice about signing any such contracts.

Many fraudulent credit repair companies are now offering to provide consumers with different business tax identification numbers (e.g., EINs) or new social security

Urban Legend Number 22: A CREDIT REPAIR AGENCY CAN IMMEDIATELY RAISE MY CREDIT SCORE.

numbers (SSN) in order to create a new credit file. This practice, called "file segregation," is illegal, and it doesn't work anyway as your new credit files will eventually be connected to your original credit files.

In this fraudulent type of action, the credit repair company asks you to apply for an Employer Identification Number (EIN) from the Internal Revenue Service (IRS), or a new social security number from the Social Security Administration. Because you made the request, you actually have the liability for the fraud instead of the credit repair company. EINs are used by businesses to report financial information to the IRS and the Social Security Administration.

Such actions are *illegal,* and may subject you to criminal penalties including fines and jail time in state or federal prisons. So please, do NOT try them. Any request for you to engage in such actions should be considered a warning sign that the company is engaging in scam activities.

You can find additional information on credit repair scams provided by the FTC online at: (ftc.gov/bcp/edu/pubs/consumer/credit/cre13.shtm).

If you have been scammed by a credit repair company, you can contact the National Fraud Information Center (NFIC) online at (www.fraud.org) or by telephone at (800)876-7060. The NFIC is a private, nonprofit organization that operates as a consumer assistance center to provide services and help in filing fraud complaints with various government agencies.

Anyone with a large amount of credit card debt can benefit from credit counseling or debt management counseling (see **Urban Legend 24**).

A low credit score is not the end of the world. A credit score is *dynamic* and can always be raised over time. Remember, *you are more than your credit score*™ (see **Urban Legend 25**).

Plastic Reactions:

- If your credit score is low, how does that make you feel?
- How do you feel about the decisions, choices and events that led you to this credit score?
- Would you do anything differently regarding those decisions, choices and events if you had the opportunity to go back and do it again?
- What can you do to improve your decisions about credit card use in the future?
- If you wish to improve your credit score, what emotions are motivating you to make that improvement?
- If you have already spoken with a credit repair agency, how did their claims make you feel? Do you feel differently now that you have read this chapter?

Urban Legend Number 22: A CREDIT REPAIR AGENCY CAN IMMEDIATELY RAISE MY CREDIT SCORE.

- How would you feel if your credit score were dramatically improved?

URBAN LEGEND – 23

I can always pay off my credit card debt by making only the minimum payment.

Urban Legend Number 23: I have made a large number of purchases on my credit card and am close to my credit limit. I am making only the minimum payment each month. I will easily be able to pay off my credit card balance over time by making just the minimum payment.

The Reality: _False._

Making only a minimum payment each month is a serious _financial debt trap_ that is a pitfall for a large number of credit card holders. It becomes a _financial death trap_ for many.

Paying only a minimum payment can keep you in debt for a very, very, long time. If you pay only a minimum payment and continue to use your credit card, you may <u>never</u> be able to pay off your balance because of your interest charges.

If you only make a minimum payment AND you continue to use your credit card, the time it will take to pay off your entire balance will be significantly longer with significantly higher interest charges. If your new purchases are equal to your payments on your principal balance, you will never lower your balance.

If you only make a minimum payment each month, and you never use your credit card again to incur additional debt, it will take you years to pay off your outstanding balance and you will incur a significant amount of interest charges.

It takes so long to pay off a credit card because credit card issuers charge _compound interest_ on credit card balances. Compound interest arises when interest is added to the principal balance. From that moment on, the interest that has been added also incurs interest charges during the next billing cycle.

However, if you make more than the minimum payment each month, you can significantly reduce the amount of time it takes to pay off your balance and the amount of interest you are charged.

As an example, assume you have a credit card balance of $5,000 and your APR is 13 percent. Your monthly finance charge for your outstanding balance will be about 1.1 percent (13 percent/12 months = 1.0833 percent per month). Assume your minimum payment is calculated using 2.0 percent of your outstanding balance.

Your first minimum payment will be $100 (0.02 x $5,000). Your finance charge will be $55 (0.011 x $5,000). Of the $100 minimum payment you made, only $45 goes to lower your balance and $55 is your interest charge. That is, your principal component payment is $45 and your interest component payment is $55.

The next month, your credit card balance will be $4,955 ($5,000 − $45). Your minimum payment will be $99.10 (0.02 x $4,955 = $99.10). Your finance charge will be $54.51 (0.011 x $4,955 = $54.51). So, of the $99.10 minimum payment, only $44.59 goes to lower your balance and $54.51 is your interest charge.

This monthly cycle continues 248 times. Not until you reach your 184th payment, about 15 years and 4 months later, does the principal component of your monthly payment exceed your interest payment portion (principal component $10.02 and interest component $9.98).

This example and the tools used on the Bills website at (www.bills.com) assume that a value for the minimum payment will always be at $20.00. In other words, even though your actual minimum payment at some point in time will be less than $20.00, a $20.00 minimum payment is always made until the entire balance is paid off. The $20.00 minimum payment level is reached at about the 176th payment made, at about 14 years and 6 months after making the first minimum payment.

If you continue to make only the minimum payment, it would take you about 20 years and 8 months to pay off your entire balance, and you would have paid over $5,175 in interest charges. You would have paid your credit card issuer a total of about $10,175 ($5,175 interest + $5,000 principal) for your original $5,000 balance.

Let us now assume that you missed your minimum payment and were charged a $35.00 late fee. In addition, your APR increases to 29 percent, based on your credit card agreement. Your monthly finance charge for your outstanding balance will be about 2.4 percent (29 percent/12 months = 2.416 percent per month). Assume also that your minimum payment after a missed payment is now calculated using 1.0 percent plus all interest and late fees of your outstanding balance. The change in interest rate and the change in minimum payment are typical of many credit card issuers.

Your outstanding balance is now $5,090 ($5,000 + $35 late fee + interest charges before late fees). Your monthly payment is now $173.91(0.01 x $5,090 + 0.024 x $5,090) and your finance charge is now $123.01 ($173.91 – $50.90).

With just one late payment and no others, it will now take you about 22 years and 3 months to pay off your credit card balance and you will now pay your credit card issuer $11,329.98 in interest and a total of $16,420 for your original $5,000 balance.

In this example, with the additional charges for late fees and the higher interest rate, the $20.00 minimum payment level is not reached until at about the 217th payment made, or at about 18 years after making the first minimum payment.

If you miss more than one payment, there is a chance you may NEVER, ever be able to pay off your credit card by making only the minimum payment.

Polly's Pearls of Wisdom: The CARD Act of 2009 now requires credit card issuers to clearly print *late payment warnings, minimum payment warnings,* and information about *credit counseling* on the front of your credit card statement.

The late payment warning section includes the late fees (e.g., $35.00 or more) and your penalty APR (e.g., 29 percent or more). The minimum payment warning section includes a table that indicates how many months or years it will take you to pay off your balance if you make only the minimum payment and what your estimated total with the interest will be.

Using the example of $5,000 balance, when the card is not used for any additional purchases and no late payments are made, the minimum payment table will look something like what is illustrated in Table 7.

Table 7. Monthly payment calculator		
If you make no additional charges using this card and each month you pay...	You will pay off the balance shown on this statement in about...	And you will end up paying an estimated total of...
Only the minimum payment	20 years, 8 months	$10,175
Fixed payment of $100/month	6 years, 1 month	$7,241
Fixed payment of $150/month	3 years, 6 months	$6,237
Fixed payment of $200/month	2 years, 6 months	$5,863

Many of these tables also include additional rows, which include values for more than the minimum payment (e.g., values for paying double or triple the minimum payment). The content of the additional rows depend on the credit card issuer.

If you are able to pay double or triple the minimum payment, or if you can work a fixed payment into your budget, you could reduce the time to pay off your balance by a large number of years — even decades — and save yourself several thousand to tens of thousands of dollars in interest charges.

For example, (as shown in Table 7) for the $5,000 balance example, if you paid $200 every month as a fixed payment (instead of the minimum payment of $100 in the beginning and smaller minimum payments each month), you would pay off your credit card balance in about 2 years and 6 months and your total payments would be about $5,863. This is a savings in time of over 18 years and about $4,312 ($10,175 – $5,863) in interest charges!

Even if you can only budget for a fixed payment of $100 per month, your payment time will be reduced by over 14 years, and you will save $2,935 in interest charges.

Making only a minimum payment will likely lower your credit score because it affects your *credit utilization* (30 percent of your credit score).

The impact of credit utilization on your credit score varies depending on your credit history (see **Urban Legend 7**).

Urban Legend Number 23: I CAN ALWAYS PAY OFF MY CREDIT CARD DEBT BY MAKING ONLY THE MINIMUM PAYMENT.

The impact of a *single missed payment* on your credit score (payment history is 35 percent of your credit score) varies depending on your credit history (see **Urban Legend 8**).

If all you can make is your minimum payment, consider transferring your balance to another credit card issuer who is offering a zero percent interest rate (see **Urban Legend 9**). Such a transfer can save you a significant amount of money in interest charges.

Free credit card minimum payment calculators and other credit card related and interest calculators can be found online at websites such as Bank Rate (www.bankrate.com), Bills (www.bills.com) and Daily Finance (www.dailyfinance.com).

If you generate a large credit card balance and cannot make the minimum payments, you should think about credit counseling (see **Urban Legend 24**). Credit card statements also list a toll-free number for credit counseling services at (866)797-2885. In some situations, you may have to consider declaring bankruptcy (see **Urban Legend 14**).

Plastic Reactions:

- How did you feel when you realized that making just a minimum payment on your credit card balance can take years, or even decades, to completely pay off your debt?

- Have you ever been in a situation in which you paid just the minimum amount due on your credit card balance? How did that decision make you feel?
- Have you ever been in a situation in which you paid off your credit card balance in full? What emotions did you experience then?
- How did you feel when you realized that missing a payment or making a late payment may put you in a situation in which you may never be able to pay off your credit card balance?
- Have you ever missed a payment or made a late payment on a credit card balance? How did that feel?
- After reading the information about how much time and money can be saved by making a larger payment on your account, will you re-think your credit card payment strategy?

Urban Legend Number 23: I CAN ALWAYS PAY OFF MY CREDIT CARD DEBT BY MAKING ONLY THE MINIMUM PAYMENT.

URBAN LEGEND – 24

Credit counseling can never help me in my current financial situation.

Urban Legend Number 24: I made a number of purchases for items I did not really need. I have a large credit card balance. I am having trouble making my minimum payment on my credit card balance. I am embarrassed to ask for help. Credit counseling or debt management counseling would not help me in my situation.

The Reality: _False._

Anyone with a large amount of credit card debt can benefit from credit counseling or debt management counseling.

Do NOT be afraid to ask for help! Not asking for help can quickly make a bad, but salvageable, financial situation into an un-salvageable situation.

Common warning signs that you are likely to need credit counseling or debt management counseling include:

- You do not have enough money to cover all the monthly payments for all your living expenses;
- You're taking out cash advances from your credit cards to cover your bills;
- You constantly try to borrow money from friends or family members to pay your bills; or
- You do not have enough money to pay your minimum payments on your credit cards.

There are a number of credit counseling and debt management services. Some will assist you for free and others will charge a fee.

Credit counselors typically assist in you with analyzing your current financial situation. They provide you with personalized long-term and short-term options based on your financial goals, and recommend the optimal debt management plans that allow you to achieve financial stability over time.

Debt management counselors typically assist you with simplifying and streamlining your debt obligations. They help you create long-term and short-term debt management plans. Many debt management counseling services also provide debt consolidation programs in which you pay a fixed monthly fee to the debt consolidation program and the program disburses funds to all your creditors on your behalf.

Polly's Pearls of Wisdom: Never, ever, be afraid to ask for help. No matter what excuses you may be making or want to make, there are a large number of credit and debt counseling services that can assist you and get you back on track to a stable and prosperous financial future.

As was first discussed for **Urban Legend 8**, if you are having trouble paying off your credit card debt, a good place to start would be to call the National Foundation for Credit Counseling (NFCC).

Urban Legend Number 24: CREDIT COUNSELING CAN NEVER HELP ME IN MY CURRENT FINANCIAL SITUATION.

The NFCC is a non-profit agency with credit counseling experts who are specifically trained to help you reduce your debt. For more information on NFCC credit counseling, visit (www.nfcc.org) or call (800)388-2227.

Also, beware of credit repair offers (see **Urban Legend 22**) which may be made by some credit counseling agencies. The Federal Reserve (www.federalreserve.gov/creditcard/manage.html), the FTC (www.ftc.gov/bcp/edu/pubs/consumer/credit/cre26.shtm) and the US Department of Justice (www.justice.gov/ust/eo/bapcpa/ccde/cc_approved) all provide information and lists of approved credit counseling and debt counseling management providers.

The FTC offers a very informative article on their website called "Knee Deep in Debt" (www.ftc.gov/bcp/edu/pubs/consumer/credit/cre19) to help people who are facing financial crisis. The article offers tips for budgeting, guides for selecting a credit counseling service, and information about debt management and settlement.

There are also a number of other for-profit and non-profit counseling agencies. Before paying any fees to a counseling agency, check the websites of the Better Business Bureau (www.bbb.org), the FTC, the Federal Reserve, and the US Department of Justice to make sure it is a legitimate credit counseling or debt management counseling agency.

Plastic Reactions:

- How much stress and negative emotions do you feel if you are/were considering credit counseling or debt management counseling?
- What additional negative emotions are/were you feeling if you thought that credit or debt management counseling couldn't help you? Now that you have read this chapter, have those feelings changed?
- If you have already contacted a credit or debt management counselor, how much stress do you feel now compared to your stress level before contacting them?
- Did you experience any positive emotions related to speaking with a credit or debt management counselor? If so, which ones?
- Did you develop a plan to take back control of your finances and to work towards a better financial future? If so, did you experience a sense of relief?

Urban Legend Number 24: CREDIT COUNSELING CAN NEVER HELP ME IN MY CURRENT FINANCIAL SITUATION.

URBAN LEGEND – 25

I should never judge myself or others by a credit score.

Urban Legend Number 25: I should never judge myself or others by a credit score!

The Reality: <u>*True.*</u>

Your credit scores are just numbers that provide one measure of your creditworthiness. *You are more than your credit score*™.

A high credit score does not make you a good person, and a low credit score does not make you a bad person.

Unfortunately, we live in a society in which value is placed on comparisons with others. The activity of comparing your credit score with the credit score of others is often a major negative emotional trigger that may cause a large drop in a person's self-esteem.

If you have a low credit score, you may feel you are not good enough, successful enough, strong enough, capable enough, or smart enough when compared to others who have a higher credit score.

Comparison is a choice and it can be unlearned. You can always improve your credit score no matter how bad it is. So stop using your credit score as a measure of comparison to anything or anybody.

Just remember, *You Are Not Your Credit Score*®. *You are more than your credit score*™.

**Polly's Pearls of Wisdom:** Impulse shopping, health emergencies, the loss of a job, a change in life situation due to a marriage, divorce or a death, and other

factors often contribute to a decline in credit score for many credit card holders.

A credit score is dynamic. It can change, and it frequently does change as life circumstances change. If you have a low credit score, do not get discouraged. Instead, view the situation from an empowered position, which gives you an opportunity to take control and initiate change. Then, make a plan with action steps you can accomplish to change to your credit card purchasing and debt management practices.

You might also consider a holistic approach to improving your credit score, including physical, psychological, emotional, and spiritual components of credit and debt management. Such an approach may result in empowering, uplifting, and life changing experiences for you and a rise in your credit score (see **You Are Not Your Credit Score**® section).

When you take these steps, your *credit-ability* and your credit score will be very different. We can see it *in the cards*!

Urban Legend Number 25: I SHOULD NEVER JUDGE MYSELF OR OTHERS BY A CREDIT SCORE.

Think for a moment and identify all the negative emotions you experience if you have a low credit score and if you are using it as a method of comparison to other people.

Plastic Reactions:

Are you feeling:
- Helpless?
- Angry?
- Frustrated?
- Sad?
- Confused?

Understanding what you're feeling will help you regain control over the situation and keep you from even more negative feelings.

Also, go back and identify all the negative emotional triggers and events that caused your credit score to go down.

- What were the emotions that went into the decisions you made that led to your lowered credit score?
- What would your reaction to those triggers or events be now?
- Would your reactions be different or the same, knowing what you know now about your credit?

AVAILABILITY OF EXTERNAL INFORMATION

Throughout this book we have included a large number of *reference indicators* to allow you to access more information about credit card topics.

The reference indicators in *The Plastic Effect* include Uniform Resource Locators (URLs) (e.g., www.theplasticeffect.com) for websites and individual web pages (e.g., www.coconutavenue.com/pollyb) on the Internet, telephone numbers, and physical street addresses for credit card and legal information. Every effort has been made to provide accurate reference indicators.

However, due to the rapidly changing nature of information on the Internet, reference indicators in this book may become out-of-date.

If you are trying to access an individual page on the Internet (e.g., www.coconutavenue.com/pollyb) and the page is gone, try accessing the website directly (e.g., www.coconutavenue.com) and searching for the same information.

You can also use a search engine to search for such information on the same website or other websites. Individual web pages are frequently moved or renamed.

If you are trying to use a reference indicator for information such as a telephone number or physical address that may become outdated, you can consult a search engine, a telephone book, call directory information from your phone, etc., to obtain current reference information.

All of the reference indicators used in this book are available at (www.coconutavenue.com/pe) and will be verified on a regular basis. Please check this webpage if you are having trouble with any of the reference indicators used in this book.

REFERENCE INFORMATION DISCLAIMER

The reference indicators included in this book are for general information purposes only. The information on these external sources can be used to deepen your knowledge of the use and misuse of your credit cards and help empower you and the financial decisions you make.

However, we have no control over the accuracy, nature, content, or availability of information on any of these external sources. The inclusion of a reference indicator to any external source does not imply any recommendation or endorsement of the goods or services provided by the external source, the accuracy of the information, or the views expressed on the external source.

We make no representations or warranties of any kind, express or implied, about the completeness, accuracy, reliability, suitability or availability with respect to the information obtained from any external source or the information, products, or services included therewith for any purpose.

Any reliance you place on such information from any external source is therefore strictly at your own risk.

PLASTIC REACTIONS DISCLAIMER

The information in the *Plastic Reactions** section is intended only to deepen your knowledge of the use and misuse of your credit cards and help empower you to make good financial decisions. Any reliance you place on such information is therefore strictly at your own risk.

If you feel that you are in need of resolving any deep-seated issues associated with the use or misuse of your credit cards that may have been raised by any of the "Plastic Reactions" questions, it may be appropriate for you to seek the counsel of a physician, licensed therapist, licensed counselor, social worker, or mental health professional.

None of the information provided in the "Plastic Reactions" sections is intended to provide any medical, psychiatric, psychological, social work, or any type of professional advice. None of the information is intended to replace or substitute for any relationship that exists, or any information, opinions, recommendations, advice, or counseling provided by any medical, psychiatric, psychological, counseling, or social work provider and a patient or a client.

Any reliance you place on such information from any "Plastic Reactions" section is therefore strictly at your own risk.

---

* PLASTIC REACTIONS^{TM} is a trademark of Coconut Avenue, Inc. Unauthorized use is prohibited.

CREDIT SCORE DISCLAIMER

The credit reporting bureaus, most major credit card issuers, financial institutions, mortgage companies, etc. have all developed their own proprietary credit scoring models. Such proprietary credit scoring models are never fully published or disclosed.

As a result, any discussion of credit scores in this book is always a *best guess* estimate. It can be used to predict a reasonable range to approximate your credit score, but your own credit score may vary.

However, remember, your credit score is always directly related to your individual credit and debt activities. The same action taken by two credit card holders is likely to yield similar, but different, end results.

We make no representations or warranties of any kind, express or implied, about the completeness, accuracy, reliability, suitability, or availability, with respect to the information about any credit scores or how their values may change.

Any reliance you place on such information from any credit score information is therefore strictly at your own risk.

ABOUT THE AUTHORS – Polly A. Bauer

Polly A. Bauer, CPCS, is an internationally recognized credit card authority, business consultant, professional speaker and an award-winning author. Polly is considered by many to be "the" preeminent expert on global credit card payment operations and all forms of payment acceptance related to the Internet, direct marketing, and automated payment transactions.

In her prior CEO and management roles, Polly consulted with leading global financial service companies, supported credit card industry policy development, created industry standard systems and practices, and helped numerous businesses avoid fraud.

Polly's pioneering work in the field of credit card fraud prevention and detection performance has also made her one of the "go-to" credit card consultants by top executives in many different industries. As a merchant advocate, Polly specializes in global payment acceptance, loss prevention, international expansion for credit card acceptance, and customer payment data security.

Polly frequently speaks on both domestic and international stages as a much-sought-after professional platform speaker. She is one of a few select individuals to achieve the Certified Professional Corporate Speaker (CPCS) certification, the highest certification given by the International Association of Corporate Speakers (IACS).

Visit Polly online at: speakerpollybauer.com

ABOUT THE AUTHORS – Stephen Lesavich

Stephen Lesavich, PhD, JD, is an attorney in private practice and an award-winning author. Stephen received a Ph.D. in computer science from the Illinois Institute of Technology in Chicago and a J.D. degree from the University of Wisconsin Law School. He has also worked professionally as a software engineer and as an adjunct professor at several different universities.

As an attorney, Dr. Lesavich regularly writes, speaks, and is interviewed about legal topics related to business law and intellectual property law (patents, trademarks, and copyrights). His articles and interviews have appeared internationally in many different print and electronic publications, and he is a frequent guest on the radio.

During the course of his legal practice at several different law firms, Stephen has represented such clients as 3Com, GE Medical Systems, Hewlett-Packard, Microsoft, Nike, Open TV, Rambus, Service Master, U.S. Robotics and many others for transactional and litigation matters.

Stephen resigned his position as a partner at a large law firm in Chicago in 2002 to become an entrepreneur and to found his own law firm, which he has grown into a very successful business.

Dr. Lesavich has served on the Board of Directors for several different for-profit and not-for-profit organizations. He has served one or more terms as a member of the Board of Directors for *Willie Dixon's Blues Heaven Foundation* in Chicago. This not-for-profit organization works to preserve the legacy of blues music.

As a software engineer, Dr. Lesavich has worked professionally for AT&T Bell Laboratories and other high-tech companies where he designed software for telecommunications systems; for the infrastructure of the Internet; and for factory automation, digital control, and robotic systems. He has published a number of technical papers in the computer science arts.

Stephen is an accredited Corporate Speaker (CS) by the International Association of Corporate Speakers (IACS). Dr. Lesavich is a sought-after speaker for lectures and workshops on topics related to the law and technology.

Visit Dr. Lesavich online at: slesavich.com

YOUR SUCCESS IS IN THE CARDS™

Helping Companies Maximize Profitability in the Credit Card Game

Polly Bauer is a CEO, industry association leader, and consultant, as well as a 30-year veteran in the credit card field. Her professional keynote speeches, consulting services, and training classes can provide your organization with the latest information on credit card related topics.

Your Success is in the Cards™ Program

Polly will teach your organization cutting edge practices for:

- Identifying the biggest enemy of exceptional merchant performance at the table.
- Going all-in to find hidden gold in operations that count.
- Utilizing payment trends to guarantee a winning hand.
- Maximizing customer sales when the chips are down.
- Other card strategies for merchants to increase profitability!

With a proven track record of success with companies ranging from the Fortune 100 to mid-sized organizations, many with revenues of $500,000 or more, Polly's programs have resulted in identifying potential or actual cost savings from millions to hundreds of millions of dollars.

What the industry is saying about Polly Bauer...

"I enthusiastically recommend Polly to any organization wanting a brilliant consultant or great keynote speaker. She's one of the best!"

Scott Adams, President, HD Publishing Group

"Polly begins to ignite the audience from the moment she steps on the podium. She keeps everyone's attention and wraps up on a high note. Her speech was definitely the talk of the conference."

Edmund J. Oman, Treasurer, West Coast Floral Association

"Polly provided valuable industry information and ideas which have helped our clients improve their bottom line."

Tracy Gonzalez, Vice-President, First National Bank of Omaha

"Listening to Polly was enough to pump up anyone's energy and enthusiasm. She reset my mental outlook."

M.K. Heffler, Past Senior Vice-President, CNBC

"Polly Bauer is a masterful communicator."

Bill Gove, Past President, National Speakers Association

For more information on **Your Success is in the Cards**™, educational programs, consulting programs, and to book keynote speeches, please contact Polly at:

Polly A. Bauer, CPCS
1324 Seven Springs Boulevard, Suite #308
New Port Richey, FL 34655 USA
Email: polly@pollyabauer.com
Phone: 01.727.410.9813
Fax: 01.727.490.2933
web: www.speakerpollybauer.com

YOUR SUCCESS IS IN THE CARDS[TM] is a trademark of Polly A. Bauer. Unauthorized use is prohibited.

YOU ARE NOT YOUR CREDIT SCORE®
YOU ARE MORE THAN YOUR CREDIT SCORE™

Polly Bauer is an internationally recognized credit card authority and credit card educator.

On her journey to the top of the credit card industry, Polly faced many challenges that affected her credit score, including divorce, unemployment, single parenthood, and other hurdles. Anyone at any time in their life's journey can find themselves in a situation that adversely affects their credit score. Like Polly, you can learn how to deal with such events.

YOU ARE NOT YOUR CREDIT SCORE®
YOU ARE MORE THAN YOUR CREDIT SCORE™
Programs

Polly will teach you or your organization cutting edge practices for:

- Exploring how a "bad" credit score affects your self-esteem and self-worth.
- Identifying the negative emotions associated with a "bad" credit score.
- Identifying patterns that result in a "bad" credit score.
- Reducing stress and anxiety associated with a "bad" credit score.
- Repairing a "bad" credit score without incurring further debt.
- Providing new debt management techniques to avoid "bad" credit score in the future.

THE PLASTIC EFFECT

- Creating a holistic approach to improving your credit score, including physical, psychological, emotional and spiritual components of credit and debt management.

Polly's programs have resulted in empowering, uplifting and life-changing experiences for large numbers of individuals and organizations.

For more information on **YOU ARE NOT YOUR CREDIT SCORE®** and **YOU ARE MORE THAN YOUR CREDIT SCORE™** educational programs, consulting programs, and to book keynote speeches on this topic, please contact Polly at:

Polly A. Bauer, CPCS
1324 Seven Springs Boulevard, Suite #308
New Port Richey, FL 34655 USA
Email: polly@pollyabauer.com
Phone: 01.727.410.9813
Fax: 01.727.490.2933
web: www.speakerpollybauer.com

YOU ARE NOT YOUR CREDIT SCORE® is a registered U.S. trademark, and YOU ARE MORE THAN YOUR CREDIT SCORE™ is a trademark of Polly A. Bauer. Unauthorized use is prohibited.

222

ABOUT COCONUT AVENUE®, INC.

®

Coconut Avenue, Inc. is a publishing company founded by *Stephen Lesavich, PhD, JD* in 2007, and is located in Chicago, Illinois. Dr. Lesavich is considered by many to be a self-help pioneer and visionary.

Coconut Avenue is located on South LaSalle Street in the financial district, the heartbeat and pulse of the city of Chicago.

Coconut Avenue publishes books in a variety of genres, in most popular print and electronic formats. Coconut Avenue books are available worldwide in bookstores and on major e-booksellers on the Internet.

Visit Coconut Avenue Online:
coconutavenue.com

OTHER COCONUT AVENUE® PRODUCTS

FOR MORE INFORMATION ABOUT OTHER COCONUT AVENUE® AUTHORS, BOOKS, PRODUCTS, AND EVENTS, PLEASE CONTACT:

Coconut Avenue, Inc.
39 S. LaSalle Street, Suite 325
Chicago, Illinois 60603 USA
(312) 419.9445 (v)
(312) 896.1539 (f)
email: info@coconutavenue.com
Online: coconutavenue.com

®

Coconut Avenue®

The Creative Avenue for Best Selling Authors®, Coconut Avenue®, The Creative Avenue For Best Selling Authors® and the *Coconut Avenue graphic®*, are registered US Trademarks of Coconut Avenue, Inc. Unauthorized use is prohibited.

APPENDIX A
Contact Information

Equifax
www.equifax.com
P.O. Box 740241
Atlanta, GA 30374
(800)846-5279

Experian
www.experian.com
P.O. Box 9530
Allen, TX 75013
(800)203-7843

TransUnion
www.transunion.com
P.O. Box 6790
Fullerton, CA 92834
(800)916-8800

Federal Trade Commission
www.ftc.gov
600 Pennsylvania Avenue, NW
Washington, DC 20580
(202)326-2222

Federal Reserve Board
www.federalreserve.gov
Federal Reserve Consumer Complaints
www.FederalReserveConsumerHelp.gov
Division of Consumer and Community Affairs
20th Street and Constitution Avenue, NW
Washington, DC 20551
(202)452-3693

Free Credit Report
www.annualcreditreport.com
Annual Credit Report Request Service
P.O. Box 105281
Atlanta, GA 30348-5281
(877)322-8228

National Foundation of Credit Counseling (NFCC)
www.nfcc.org
2000 M Street
NW Suite 505
Washington, DC 20036
(202)677-4300

US Department of Justice
www.justice.gov
950 Pennsylvania Avenue, NW
Washington, DC 20530-0001
(202)514-2000

END NOTES

[1] **What is a Credit Report?** Title 15 of the United States Code, section 1681 (15 U.S.C. §1681(c)) controls the behavior of credit reporting agencies. This law is known as the Fair Credit Reporting Act (FCRA).

[2] **What is a Credit Report?** Fair and Accurate Credit Transactions Act of 2003, Public Law 108-159. See the Fair Credit Reporting Act (15 U.S.C. §1681 et seq.) (www.ftc.gov/os/statutes/031224fcra.pdf).

[3] **What is a Credit Report?** U.S. Federal Law provides (Title 16 of Code of Federal Regulations (C.F.R.) Part 610 (16 C.F.R. §610)) that upon a request by a consumer and without charge, once in any 12-month period (in compliance with section 612(a) of the FCRA (15 U.S.C. §1681(a)), the consumer can receive one copy of their credit report for free from each of the three nationwide credit reporting bureaus: *Experian, Equifax,* and *TransUnion.*

[4] **Urban Legend - 5:** H.R. 627 (111th): Credit Card Accountability and Disclosure Act of 2009. (www.govtrack.us/congress/bills/111/hr627/text).

[5] **Urban Legend - 8:** Consumer Financial Protection Bureau. 2012. "CARD Act Factsheet," published February 22, 2010, (www.consumerfinance.gov/credit-cards/credit-card-act/feb2011-factsheet/).

---

[6] **Urban Legend - 10:** The White House, Office of the Press Secretary. 2012. "Fact Sheet: Reforms to Protect American Credit Card Holders," (May 22, 2009) (www.whitehouse.gov/the_press_office/Fact-Sheet-Reforms-to-Protect-American-Credit-Card-Holders).

[7] **Urban Legend - 10:** Consumer Financial Protection Bureau. 2012. "CARD Act Factsheet," published February 22, 2010, (www.consumerfinance.gov/credit-cards/credit-card-act/feb2011-factsheet/).

[8] **Urban Legend - 10:** Consumer Financial Protection Bureau. 2012. "CARD Act Factsheet," published February 22, 2010, (www.consumerfinance.gov/credit-cards/credit-card-act/feb2011-factsheet/).

[9] **Urban Legend - 12:** US Census. 2012. "Table 132. People Who Got Married, and Divorced in the Past 12 Months by State: 2009" (www.census.gov/compendia/statab/2012/tables/12s0132.pdf).

[10] **Urban Legend - 13:** Under the FCRA §605 (a) and (b), an account in collection will appear on a consumer's credit report for 7 years. The clock starts approximately 180 days after the date of first delinquency on the account.

[11] **Urban Legend - 13:** Fontanielle, Amy. "Beware of Zombie Debt Collectors," *Investopedia* (October 31, 2008). 2012. (www.forbes.com/2008/10/31/debt-creditors-default-pf-education-in_af_1031investopedia_inl.html).

[12] **Urban Legend - 14:** US Courts. 2012. "Table F-2. US Bankruptcy Courts — Business and Non-business Cases Commenced, by Chapter of the Bankruptcy Code, During the 12-Month Period Ending December 31, 2011," (www.uscourts.gov/uscourts/Statistics/BankruptcyStatistics/BankruptcyFilings/2011/1211_f2.pdf).

[13] **Urban Legend - 14:** United States Courts. 2012. "Bankruptcy Filings Down in Fiscal Year 2012," (November 7, 2012) (news.uscourts.gov/bankruptcy-filings-down-fiscal-year-2012).

[14] **Urban Legend - 14:** Chapter 7 of Title 11 of the United States Code. 11 U.S.C. §700.

[15] **Urban Legend - 14:** Chapter 13 of Title 11 of the United States Code. 11 U.S.C. §1300.

[16] **Urban Legend - 14:** Bankruptcy 11 U.S.C. §523(a)(2)(C)(i)(I), 11 U.S.C. §1328(b).

[17] **Urban Legend - 14:** Bankruptcy 11 U.S.C. §547(b)(4)(B), 11 U.S.C. §547(c)(8), 11 U.S.C. §101(31).

[18] **Urban Legend - 14:** Bankruptcy 11 U.S.C. §727(a)(8).

[19] **Urban Legend - 18:** Federal Trade Commission, "Statement of Policy Regarding Communications in Connection With the Collection of Decedent's Debts," *Federal Register* 76, no. 144 (July 27, 2011). (ftc.gov/os/2011/07/110720fdcpa.pdf).

[20] **Urban Legend - 18:** Kübler-Ross, Elisabeth and David Kessler. 2005. *On Grief and Grieving: Finding the Meaning of Grief Through the Five Stages of Loss*, Simon & Schuster.

[21] **Urban Legend - 19:** The Federal Trade Commission. 2012. "Facts for Consumers — Equal Credit Opportunity: Understanding Your Rights Under the Law" (www.ftc.gov/bcp/edu/pubs/consumer/credit/.shtm). The **Equal Credit Opportunity Act** (ECOA) is a United States law (codified at 15 U.S.C. §1691 et seq.).

[22] **Urban Legend - 19:** Curry, Pat. 2012. "10 questions before getting secured credit cards" (www.bankrate.com/finance/credit-cards/10-questions-before-getting-a-secured-credit-card-1.aspx).

[23] **Urban Legend - 20:** National Association of State PIRGs. 2012. "Mistakes Do Happen: A Look at Errors in Consumer Credit Reports" (June 2004) (georgiapirg.org/sites/pirg/files/reports/MistakesDoHappen2004-1.pdf).

[24] **Urban Legend - 20:** Riepenhoff, Jill and Mike Wagner. "Dispatch Investigation — Credit Scars: Credit-reporting agencies' failure to address damaging errors plaguing thousands of Americans prompts call for swift action," *Columbus Dispatch* (May 6, 2012). 2012. (www.dispatch.com/content/stories/local/2012/05/06/cred it-scars.html).

[25] **Urban Legend - 20:** Singletary, Michelle. "Can't fix error in your credit report? Call Consumer Financial Protection Bureau," *Washington Post* (October 23, 2012). 2012. (www.washingtonpost.com/business/economy/cant-fix-error-in-your-credit-report-call-consumer-financial-protection-bureau/2012/10/23/09a28898-1d4b-11e2-9cd5-b55c38388962_story.html).

[26] **Urban Legend - 21:** The Federal Trade Commission. 2012. "Facts for Consumers —Fair Credit Billing" (ftc.gov/bcp/edu/pubs/consumer/credit/cre16.shtm).

[27] **Urban Legend - 21:** The Electronic Fund Transfer Act (EFTA) is a United States federal law (codified at 15 U.S.C. §1601 et seq.) (www.fdic.gov/regulations/laws/rules/6500-1350.html).

[28] **Urban Legend - 21:** Regulation E, pursuant to the Electronic Fund Transfer Act (EFTA), 12 C.F.R. §205.6 sets liability of consumer for unauthorized transfers (www.fdic.gov/regulations/laws/rules/6500-3100.html#fdic6500205.6).

[29] **Urban Legend - 21:** The Federal Trade Commission. 2012. "Facts for Consumers — Credit, ATM and Debit Cards: What to Do if They're Lost or Stolen" (ftc.gov/bcp/edu/pubs/consumer/credit/cre04.shtm). The Fair Credit Billing Act (FCBA) is a United States federal law enacted in 1975 as an amendment to the Truth in Lending Act (codified at 15 U.S.C. §1601 et seq.).

[30] **Urban Legend - 22:** The Federal Trade Commission. 2012. "Chapter 2 — Credit Repair Organizations (1), Sec 2451. Regulation of Credit Repair Organizations." (www.ftc.gov/os/statutes/croa/croa.shtm).

END NOTES

The Plastic Effect
2013 Independent Publisher Living Now
Book Award Winner

Recognizing the Year's Best Books for Better Living
Gold Medal Winner
Judged Best New Book in the Finance/Budgeting Category

"The Independent Publisher Living Now Book Awards celebrate the innovation and creativity of newly published books that enhance the quality of our lives and publicize the importance of these books to readers and their vitality in the marketplace."

COCONUT AVENUE®, INC.

AN AWARD WINNING PUBLISHING COMPANY

Coconut Avenue, Inc. was selected for the **2014 Best of Chicago Award** in *the Publishing Consultants & Services* category by the Chicago Award Program.

"The Chicago Award Program recognizes companies that enhance the positive image of small business through exceptional service to their customers and their community. These award-winning companies help make the Chicago area a great place to live, work and play.

®

Coconut
AVENUE, INC.

If you are interested in discussing current credit card topics,

please join Polly Bauer (@CreditCrdQueen) and Stephen Lesavich

(@SLesavich) on Twitter at the hash tag, **#THEPLASTICEFFECT**.

www.ingramcontent.com/pod-product-compliance
Lightning Source LLC
Chambersburg PA
CBHW031808190326
41518CB00006B/242